Alexander Denecke

Hypothesis-based image segmentation

Alexander Denecke

Hypothesis-based image segmentation
A Machine Learning Approach

Südwestdeutscher Verlag für Hochschulschriften

Impressum/Imprint (nur für Deutschland/only for Germany)
Bibliografische Information der Deutschen Nationalbibliothek: Die Deutsche Nationalbibliothek verzeichnet diese Publikation in der Deutschen Nationalbibliografie; detaillierte bibliografische Daten sind im Internet über http://dnb.d-nb.de abrufbar.
Alle in diesem Buch genannten Marken und Produktnamen unterliegen warenzeichen-, marken- oder patentrechtlichem Schutz bzw. sind Warenzeichen oder eingetragene Warenzeichen der jeweiligen Inhaber. Die Wiedergabe von Marken, Produktnamen, Gebrauchsnamen, Handelsnamen, Warenbezeichnungen u.s.w. in diesem Werk berechtigt auch ohne besondere Kennzeichnung nicht zu der Annahme, dass solche Namen im Sinne der Warenzeichen- und Markenschutzgesetzgebung als frei zu betrachten wären und daher von jedermann benutzt werden dürften.

Coverbild: www.ingimage.com

Verlag: Südwestdeutscher Verlag für Hochschulschriften GmbH & Co. KG
Heinrich-Böcking-Str. 6-8, 66121 Saarbrücken, Deutschland
Telefon +49 681 37 20 271-1, Telefax +49 681 37 20 271-0
Email: info@svh-verlag.de

Approved by: Bielefeld, Diss., 2011

Herstellung in Deutschland (siehe letzte Seite)
ISBN: 978-3-8381-3371-3

Imprint (only for USA, GB)
Bibliographic information published by the Deutsche Nationalbibliothek: The Deutsche Nationalbibliothek lists this publication in the Deutsche Nationalbibliografie; detailed bibliographic data are available in the Internet at http://dnb.d-nb.de.
Any brand names and product names mentioned in this book are subject to trademark, brand or patent protection and are trademarks or registered trademarks of their respective holders. The use of brand names, product names, common names, trade names, product descriptions etc. even without a particular marking in this works is in no way to be construed to mean that such names may be regarded as unrestricted in respect of trademark and brand protection legislation and could thus be used by anyone.

Cover image: www.ingimage.com

Publisher: Südwestdeutscher Verlag für Hochschulschriften GmbH & Co. KG
Heinrich-Böcking-Str. 6-8, 66121 Saarbrücken, Germany
Phone +49 681 37 20 271-1, Fax +49 681 37 20 271-0
Email: info@svh-verlag.de

Printed in the U.S.A.
Printed in the U.K. by (see last page)
ISBN: 978-3-8381-3371-3

Copyright © 2012 by the author and Südwestdeutscher Verlag für Hochschulschriften GmbH & Co. KG and licensors
All rights reserved. Saarbrücken 2012

Para Irene . . .

Contents

1 **Introduction**   1
    1.1 Scope and contribution of the thesis 4
    1.2 Thesis outline 6

2 **Motivation of figure-ground segmentation**   9
    2.1 Background 9
        2.1.1 Concepts of biologically motivated computer vision 10
        2.1.2 A system view: The technical role of object segmentation 15
        2.1.3 Summary 19
    2.2 Computational models 19
        2.2.1 Color image segmentation 20
        2.2.2 Foreground segmentation 23
    2.3 Discussion 32

3 **A learning vector quantization approach**   35
    3.1 Introduction 36
    3.2 Generalized Learning Vector Quantization 36
        3.2.1 Adaptive metrics in GLVQ 38
    3.3 Application of GLVQ for image segmentation 40
        3.3.1 Algorithm 42
        3.3.2 Relevant properties of the model 43
    3.4 Simulations 45
        3.4.1 Evaluation 46
        3.4.2 Evaluation of adaptive metrics in GLVQ 47

- 3.4.3 Hypothesis-based segmentation 50
- 3.4.4 Effect of feature weighting 52
- 3.4.5 Robustness with respect to hypothesis placement 54
- 3.5 Summary 56

4 Integrated vision systems 59
- 4.1 Introduction 60
- 4.2 Vision systems for human-robot interaction 61
  - 4.2.1 HRI research platform 62
  - 4.2.2 Data acquisition and preprocessing 63
  - 4.2.3 Figure-ground segmentation 65
- 4.3 Feature extraction methods 65
  - 4.3.1 The feed-forward feature hierarchy 66
  - 4.3.2 The analytic feature approach 68
- 4.4 Simulations 71
  - 4.4.1 BASS: View-based object learning and recognition 71
  - 4.4.2 BRAVO-1: Parts-based object recognition 75
- 4.5 Discussion 78

5 The model selection problem 81
- 5.1 Introduction 82
- 5.2 Online figure-ground segmentation with adaptive network dimensionality 83
- 5.3 Simulations 87
  - 5.3.1 Experimental Setup 87
  - 5.3.2 Results 88
- 5.4 Summary 89

6 Discriminative region modeling in level set methods and graph cuts 91
- 6.1 Introduction 92
- 6.2 Methods 93
  - 6.2.1 Level-set segmentation methods 93
  - 6.2.2 Graph cuts for image segmentation 95

	6.3	Integration of LGMLVQ	98
		6.3.1 Level set formulation	98
		6.3.2 Graph cuts formulation	99
	6.4	Simulations	100
		6.4.1 Experimental setup	100
		6.4.2 Model parameter	102
		6.4.3 Results	104
	6.5	Discussion	105
	6.6	Summary	109

7 Conclusion — 111
7.1 Outlook — 113

A Notation — 115

B Abreviations — 117

C Datasets — 119
C.1 PBD: Public benchmark data — 119
C.2 HRIR25: HRI dataset of rendered objects — 119
C.3 HRI50: Data from human-robot interaction — 120
C.4 HRI126: Data from human-robot interaction — 120
C.5 CAR: Data from car the detection scenario — 120

D Results — 127
D.1 Image segmentation for CAR dataset — 127
D.2 Image segmentation for HRI50 dataset — 127

E Acknowledgments — 147

Chapter 1

Introduction

The aim of this chapter is to motivate this thesis with an overview about the scientific context, namely the research on cognitive robotics. In this field classical research topics are the construction of robotic systems, their sensory capabilities and the control of their actuators in order to enable the interaction with the environment. In an industrial application like assembling a car, a preprogrammed and repetitive behavior of the system is sufficient to fulfill a certain task with high precision and efficiency. Contrary the development on cognitive systems is driven by the intention to construct a versatile robot that can be used in dynamically changing and even novel situations. In fact, robotics in general is supposed to be a key technology for our future with increasing relevance in applications for the household or for entertainment (McMail 2009; Gates 2007). These scenarios cannot be constrained like an assembly line and consequently a subject of current research is to endow artificial systems with a flexible and intelligent behavior in their complex and changing environment.

The understanding of biological systems is a possible basis for the development of new concepts to face future challenges. It is widely assumed that learning is one of the fundamental abilities that distinguish artificial systems from the biological counterparts. Cognitive robotics addresses the acquisition and usage of knowledge with respect to motor skills or sensory capabilities to make possible that an artificial system can adapt its behavior according to the situation and past experience. The processing of visual information is fundamental, e.g. for the visual localization, navigation and the recognition of physical objects in the environment. Relevant questions with respect to the acquisition of visual knowledge are how to represent a huge number of visual objects, how to discriminate between them and to recognize known objects also in new visual context. But sensory processing cannot be simply decoupled from the whole system and visual learning has to be investigated in the context of an interaction of the system with its environment or human tutors (Arsenio 2004b). To illustrate this, Fig. 1.1 displays

 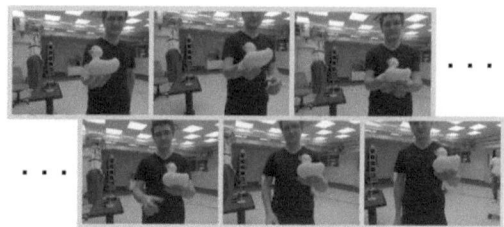

Figure 1.1: *The left image shows a typical human-robot interaction, where a human tutor presents an object to an artificial vision system. This scenario is unconstrained in the sense that learning and recognition takes place in a dynamical scene. That is, the tutor presents the object by hand from an arbitrary viewing position in front of a cluttered background. On the right, a short sequence of frames from the system perspective is presented, demonstrating the interaction scenario.*

a human-robot interaction showing the typical setup as well as the view from the system perspective. Such complex interaction can be characterized by a human tutor in front of a dynamically changing and cluttered background. The object of interest is showed by hand and is freely rotated during the presentation. To enable learning in such scenario the system has to determine where the behaviorally relevant parts of the scene are and which image regions belong to a particular physical entity.

It was already recognized that the handling of unconstrained and changing environments are an important problem for future work (Arsenio and Fitzpatrick 2005). With respect to the problem, "where" in the scene is something to learn, a priori the system has no clue which parts of the image are relevant for learning. Furthermore, in the initial learning phase we cannot assume an already acquired representation, i.e. the appearance of the objects is unknown. In this case an external clue is necessary to guide the attention of the system to a particular location in the scene in order to bootstrap the learning procedure. Models to determine salient image regions offer a possibility to provide such clue. In (Walther et al. 2005) a bottom-up saliency model (Itti et al. 1998) was used in combination with a method to determine a region of interest around the most salient location in the image. Nevertheless the derived image regions only correspond very roughly to an object. For this reason, current systems for object learning and recognition also integrate simple segmentation concepts. In some cases they work on monochromatic background or they directly use cues like motion or stereo disparity to obtain the relevant object regions. In (Björkmann and Eklundh 2004; Kim et al. 2006) object learning systems are presented that rely on a combination of an attention system with stereo disparity depth cue to segment the object from the background. To guide the attention of the system the concept of shared attention can also be used. A motion based segmentation model

(a) (b) (c)

Figure 1.2: *Segmentation problem: the system has to determine the behaviorally relevant parts of the scene and which image regions belong to a particular physical entity. In general the decomposition of a visual scene (a) into its constituents (b) is a subjective and task-dependent problem. Figure-ground segmentation follows a simplified concept to decompose the scene into a relevant object and its surrounding background (c).*

was proposed in (Arsenio 2004a). Here a human teacher drives the robot through the process of segmenting objects from arbitrarily complex non-static images. The method proposed in (Goerick et al. 2005) combines several aspects of the models mentioned before. An attention system that rely on three levels, bottom-up attention, motion detection and depth estimation to detect behaviorally relevant stimuli and segment them from the background. This system was the basis for further work on the general concept of proto-objects (Bolder et al. 2007). According to (Schmüdderich 2010) these proto-objects are understood as

> ... a representation of objects in the environment, with the important property that they lack any appearance, or concept dependence, but rather act as an unspecific, general pointer to the object.

In other words a proto-object is a general concept of an object in the scene that is defined by coherence of unconditional cues, such as depth or motion. Therefore this concept comprises the methods mentioned before as special concept that rely only on a single cue. Such methods primarily address the question where "something interesting" is in the visual scene. But these methods only partially address the question what is related to a certain object or physical entity. The cues provided by motion and depth estimation are hard to estimate on homogenously colored regions and therefore may be only partially available. Additionally depth estimation can only give a coarse approximation of the object outline due to the ill-posed task to recover 3D information from 2D data.

The task to determine which image regions belong to a particular object is referred as the image segmentation problem (Fig. 1.2). Image segmentation is one of the most challenging tasks in computer vision and a crucial concept in multiple applications. Subject of this thesis is the special case of figure-ground segmentation, which is the process that separates the image into two regions, the object of interest and the background clutter. This process serves as preprocessing step for machine learning techniques to separate the visual features of the object from the features occurring in the background. Regarding subsequent object learning, this step is necessary in order to determine the visual properties of objects, such as their shape for instance. Furthermore a figure-ground segmentation allows the application of object recognition methods in unconstrained environment with cluttered background and increases their efficiency by constraining the computation to the relevant location of the image. In other words, a figure-ground segmentation separates the object identity and the location in the scene i.e. achieves invariance to the stimulus position.

1.1 Scope and contribution of the thesis

The goal of this thesis is to overcome the limitations of visual learning in human-robot interaction by separating the object of interest from the background. Current state-of-the-art methods are restricted to simplified scenarios or suffer from suboptimal learning performance due to cluttered training data. Therefore this work addresses figure-ground segmentation as a basis to investigate algorithms for visual learning, where we want to demonstrate that such concept improves human-robot interaction and real-time object recognition. The context of the work, e.g. the online-learning in changing and unpredictable environmental conditions, imposes significant constraints on this dissertation. The developed methods are intended to be integrated in complex artificial vision systems. Hence, the capability to process the image data in real-time is as important as the applicability in unconstrained environments with complex shaped objects presented naturally held in hand.

Research goals The first research goal is therefore defined as the analysis, development, and implementation of a figure-ground segmentation scheme that is applicable in a visual learning system. This task is in particular challenging as the method to develop has to be applied to unknown objects of complex shape and heterogeneous color and has to be robust to a dynamically changing environment. For this reasons a the second research goal addresses the trade-off between the complexity of the model and its applicability in a wide range of scenarios. That is, we aim for a method that is robust in its parameterization and against changes in the scenario. In particular in an online setup with dynamically changing difficulty of the data a predefined model complexity has only a tight range of applicability.

The third research goal comprises the integration of multiple segmentation criteria. In image

1.1. SCOPE AND CONTRIBUTION OF THE THESIS

segmentation several concepts can be used, e.g. feature-based segmentation on the basis of the color as well as the integration of higher level concepts like shape, the size of the region or the smoothness of the obtained object boundary among others. Therefore the method has to be able to respect these different segmentation criteria to obtain spatially consistent image segmentation.

All of the defined research goals are challenging in the sense that they are ill-posed. These are the image segmentation problem, the problem to estimate the number of visual entities in an image (i.e. the appropriate choice of the model complexity) and also the problem to combine multiple segmentation cues. For this reasons the success of the work will be judged on the basis of the task, the quality of the image segmentation and the impact on object learning and recognition.

Contributions Our first contribution is the analysis and application of a Learning Vector Quantization approach for figure-ground segmentation. The method is applied to object recognition data of a human-robot interaction scenario. A hypothesis-based concept is used in order to segment the objects in front of a dynamically changing and cluttered scene. In other words, the processing of what is to be segmented in the image and the segmentation itself are separated from each other. This is accomplished by providing an initial segmentation cue that is used to adapt the figure-ground segmentation.

The proposed method improves the state-of-the-art with respect to the requirements on the hypothesis as well as an integrated feature weighting mechanism to handle similar colors in foreground and background. Finally we show that object recognition systems can take a significant profit of this method compared to simple segmentation cues like motion and stereo disparity.

A second central theme of this work deals with the model selection problem of the proposed method since the Learning Vector Quantization approach is a prototype-based model. The appropriate choice of the number of model neurons is a principle problem in Vector Quantization networks and it affects the performance and the runtime of the segmentation algorithm. Because of the hypothesis-based concept the complexity of the network is also relevant regarding over-fitting effects. Incremental learning offers a solution to find a trade-off between representation quality and the avoidance of over-fitting. However, since the hypothesis can provide partially wrong information standard incremental methods to estimate the number of model neurons are not appropriate on this supervised information. Here we adopt a local criterion to estimate the utility of the prototypes and show, that the number of prototypes can be efficiently controlled by a small set of rules.

As stated before, the first contribution of this thesis addresses the development of a method to separate foreground and background on the basis of an initial hypothesis and the feature-based classification of the pixel. This model does not integrate concepts like neighboring image regions, compactness of the segmentation and shape. Therefore we investigate state-of-the-art energy minimization techniques (level set methods and graph-cuts) to combine such region-based concepts with the modeling of the image statistics by means of an artificial neural network. We show that the proposed segmentation model can be improved by taking additional optimization criteria into account. Compared to standard region modeling techniques like histograms, the neural network-based method improves state-of-the-art figure-ground segmentation schemes on the basis of these energy minimization techniques.

1.2 Thesis outline

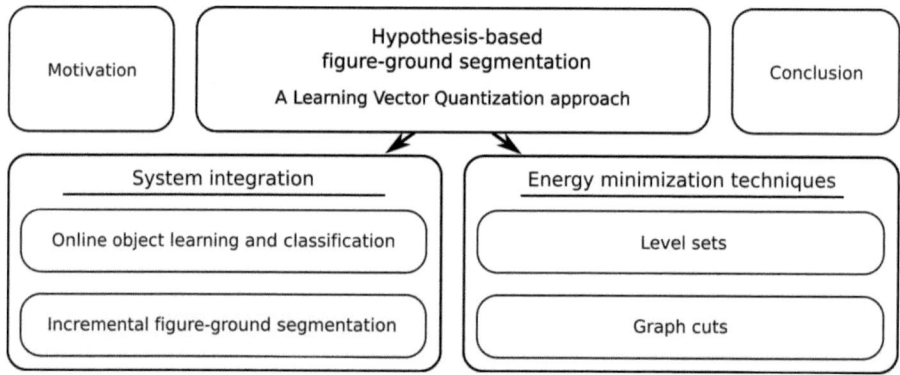

Figure 1.3: *This thesis comprises three main parts. Our central topic is a Learning Vector Quantization approach to obtain a robust figure-ground segmentation scheme. This method is applied to data of a human-robot interaction scenario in an unconstrained environment. In this context an incremental extension of the method is also proposed to ensure a broad range of applicability. Finally the method is extended towards a level set and graph cuts implementation to allow the integration of image-based segmentation concepts like spatial neighborhood or contour constraints.*

The chapters of the thesis follow the outline of the contributions denoted before and comprise three main parts (Fig. 1.3). In Chapter 2 the motivation of figure-ground segmentation and a review of state-of-the-art methods from image processing are given. We discuss the purpose of figure-ground segmentation and show that it is a crucial component for state-of-the art object learning and recognition methods. In Chapter 3 we introduce the proposed figure-ground segmentation algorithm on the basis of a Learning Vector Quantization approach. The method

1.2. THESIS OUTLINE

can be distinguished from state-of-the-art models by its robustness and feature weighting capabilities.

The second part of the presented work addresses the impact on the succeeding object learning stages. In Chapter 4 we focus on the application of the proposed method in two different scenarios for online-learning and recognition and show the benefit of the proposed figure-ground segmentation scheme. Furthermore in Chapter 5 we aim for an improvement of our method, namely the incremental adaptation of the network size that is the most important parameter and a fundamental problem in prototype-based networks.

Finally our neural network-based approach has to be linked to the state-of-the-art segmentation methods. In Chapter 6 we propose an integration with level set methods and graph cuts. Both methods for image segmentation allow an integration of further segmentation criteria. We demonstrate that the combination of the proposed algorithms produce competitive results on a common benchmark dataset and outperforms other established methods. In both cases the Learning Vector Quantization approach integrates the concept of metrics adaptation. This allows to obtain a robust region classifier that can handle complex colored objects and to determine the relevant feature dimensions in order to discriminate between foreground and background. On the other hand level set methods and graph cuts impose further region constraints and a contour optimization to obtain consistent segmentations.

Chapter 2

Motivation of figure-ground segmentation

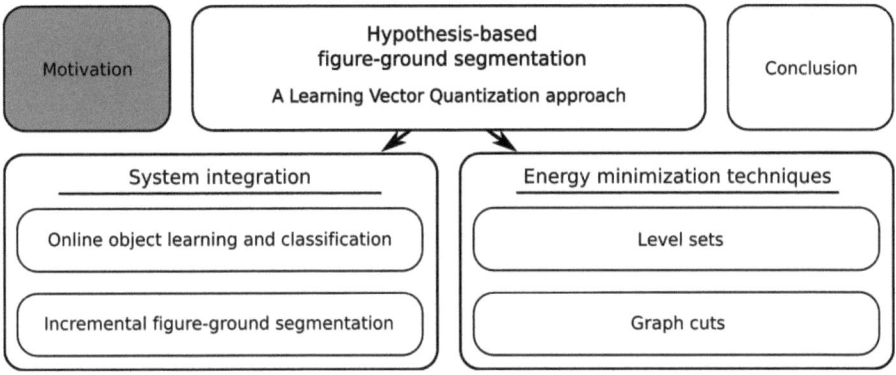

In this chapter the problem of figure-ground segmentation is motivated. We begin with an overview about the current knowledge and architectures for the representation of visual objects and the possible role of a figure-ground segmentation stage. Afterwards we review the current state-of-the-art methods for image segmentation and lead over to the special case of figure-ground segmentation. Finally we introduce the concept of hypothesis-based figure-ground segmentation, which is the basis for the remaining parts of this thesis.

2.1 Background

To introduce the figure-ground segmentation task we will address the question why such process is important in the context of visual learning. Before we discuss its necessity for computational

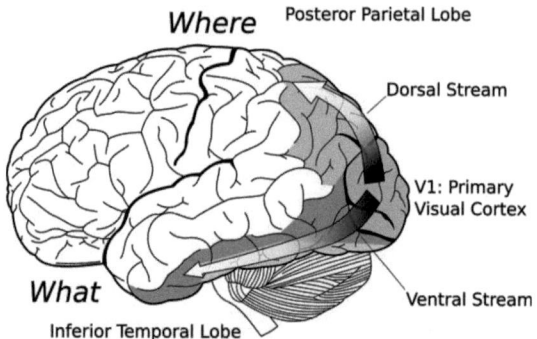

Figure 2.1: *Visual pathways[1]. The visual stimulus perceived by the retina is projected via the lateral geniculate nucleus (LGN) to the primary visual cortex (V1). According to the theory of distinct visual processing streams (Goodale and Milner 1992) the identity of the stimulus and its location in the scene are processed in different areas of the brain. The dorsal visual stream (resp. "Where"-pathway) is associated with spatial awareness and guidance of action. The ventral visual stream (resp. "What"-pathway) is associated with the recognition of the stimulus.*

approaches to object recognition, we give an overview of the current knowledge about the concepts of visual processing in the human brain.

2.1.1 Concepts of biologically motivated computer vision

According to our current knowledge about the neuronal visual processing two concepts are relevant for this thesis. The first concept comprises the separation of visual processing in two distinct and specialized processing streams (Fig.2.1). These are the ventral visual pathway for object identity and the dorsal visual pathway for spatial vision/attention (Mishkin et al. 1983; Goodale and Milner 1992). Because structures of the dorsal stream are involved in the interaction with the motor cortex for the visual guidance of actions, this distinction into dorsal and ventral stream is also known as action vs. perception (Goodale and Westwood 2004). Goodale and Westwood (2004) pointed out that

> ... *in specific situations, particularly where rapid responses to visible targets are required, visual motor control engages processing mechanisms that are quite different from those that underlie our conscious visual experience of the world.*

Due to very complex interactions between both streams (Koshino et al. 2005) this distinction often seems to be inadequate (Hamker 2002) but the separation is still a well accepted

2.1. BACKGROUND

model for visual information processing. This concept is important regarding the motivation of figure-ground segmentation. The second concept is relevant with respect to computational architectures for visual object recognition, namely that in the sensory visual cortex the neuronal information processing follows the principle from simple to complex analysis. This is reflected in the understanding of the ventral visual pathway.

Ventral visual pathway From the initial retinal perception the visual information is projected via the lateral geniculate nucleus (LGN) to the primary visual cortex V1. Then the ventral visual pathway begins in V1 and follows the visual areas V2 and V4 to the inferotemporal cortex (IT) (Ungerleider and Haxby 1994). Those visual areas explicitly represent information about color and shape with increasingly sophisticated representations. The ventral visual pathway is supposed to mediate object recognition in primates and is classically described as a feed-forward hierarchy of neurons with increasing size of the receptive fields, complexity of the represented features and invariance to stimulus variations (Fig. 2.2). On the level of V1 already a small invariance to stimulus position is achieved by the combination of simple and complex cells (Hubel and Wiesel 1962; Hubel and Wiesel 1965; Carandini 2006). Simple cells exhibited strong phase dependence (i.e. respond to edge orientation (DeValois et al. 1982)), whereas the response of complex cells can be explained by pooling together simple cells responses with similar selectivity but with translated receptive fields. Neurons in the visual area V4 are sensitive to stimuli of moderate complexity with a tuning for curvature, orientation and object-relative position of boundary fragments within larger, more complex global shapes (Pasupathy and Connor 2002; Cadieu et al. 2007). On the highest level (IT) of monomodal visual processing, neurons can be selective for complex shapes like views of objects, parts of them and their configurations (Tanaka 2003).

Dorsal visual pathway The dorsal stream starts also in the primary visual cortex and moves up through V2, V3 to medial temporal area (MT) and finally to the parietal cortex (Wang et al. 1999). This pathway is involved in spatial processing, spatially-oriented action and visual tracking (Schlesinger and Limongi 2005) and can be characterized by its high sensitivity to contrast and motion. The parietal cortex at the end of the dorsal stream is involved in the control of visual attention (Wojciulik and Kanwisher 1999) and visual saliency (VanRullen 2003). Attention through visual saliency (Itti 2000) as one aspect of dorsal processing is in particular interesting for structuring vision processes (Goerick et al. 2005). The hierarchical model from Itti, Koch, and Niebur (1998) is a well established method. Recent work (Itti and Baldi 2005; Voorhies et al. 2010) combines the ideas of saliency computation (spatial surprise) with novelty detection (temporal surprise) and allows to reliably model the gaze direction of human observers in front of complex video stimuli (see Fig. 2.3). This effort together with

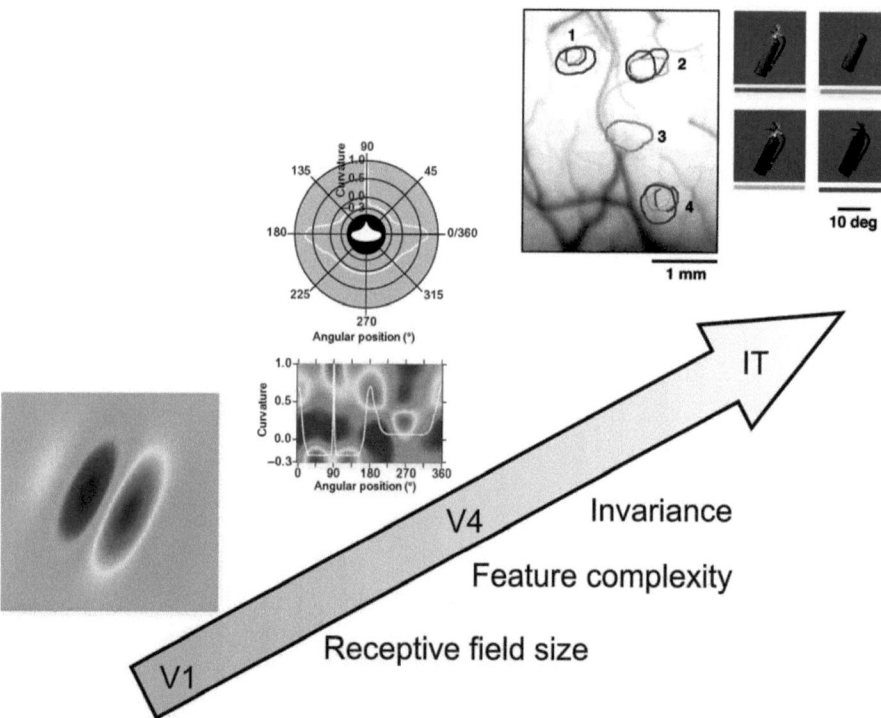

Figure 2.2: *Illustration of different stages of the ventral visual pathway. This pathway can be characterized by an increasing size of the receptive fields, increasing complexity of the features as well as an increasing invariance to stimulus variations like position and orientation (Pasupathy and Connor 2002). The ventral visual pathway is supposed to start at the primary visual cortex V1. A large amount of neurons in this area exhibited strong phase dependence that can be modeled by means of Gabor filters (Jones and Palmer 1987). The visual area V4 was selected to illustrate an intermediate stage. Here the population response to a complex shape dependent on curvature and angular position of the stimulus is displayed. Finally at the level of inferotemporal cortex (IT) the activation of populations of neurons to a complex object are shown (Tanaka 2003).*

2.1. BACKGROUND

(a)   (b)

Figure 2.3: *Example of the work of Itti and Baldi (2005). The human saccade in a natural scene (left image) is predicted by a model for visual saliency and surprise (right image).*

models of the ventral visual pathway is a promising and biologically plausible way for the recognition of multiple objects in natural scenes (Walther et al. 2005; Walther 2006).

2.1.1.1 Biological evidence for figure-ground segmentation

With respect to this model of visual processing we can ask how distinct objects can be isolated from the visual scene and subjected to the recognition process. In fact several evidences for separate processing of foreground and background exist. We can group them by their level of detail: phenomenological analysis, the neuronal level (single cell recordings) and brain imaging techniques.

Phenomenological evidence The problem of figure-ground organization is connected with the more general problem of grouping in visual perception. The perceptual organization of the visual input, i.e. which parts should be perceived together, is subject of several visual phenomena known as Gestalt rules (Wertheimer 1938; Koffka 1935; Rubin 1958). Such "rules" are for example the grouping of visual elements by proximity, similarity or common fate, see (Palmer 1999) for a comprehensive overview.

In contrast figure-ground organization bases on the perception of visual elements as belonging together in the sense of forming an object or a particular entity in the scene. Similar to the Gestalt rules several principles can be formulated on phenomenological analysis (Fig. 2.4, (Palmer 1999)). Most of those principles are formulated with respect to the shape of the object. Peterson (1999) defines the figure as something that has a definite shape and the contour is perceived as part of the figure. In fact foreground and background are perceived and memorized

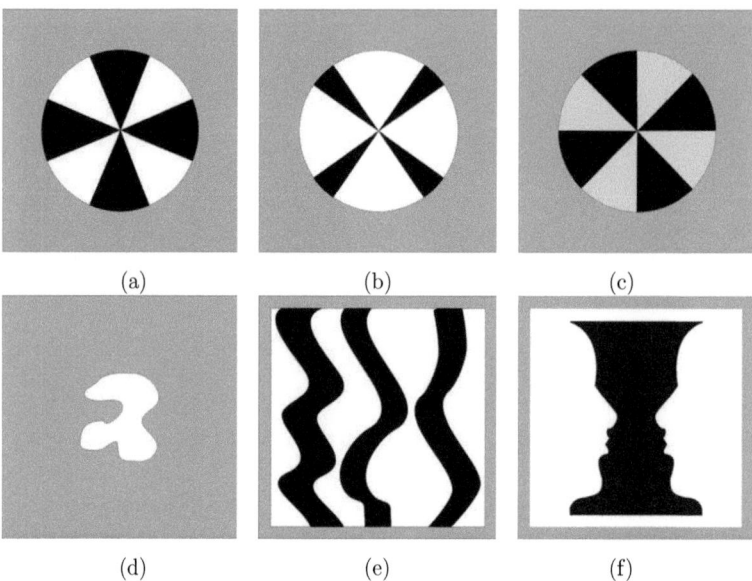

Figure 2.4: *Principles of figure-ground organization according to Palmer (1999). Regions are more frequently perceived as figure if one or more of the following criteria is fullfilled:* **Orientation** *(a) - stimuli are horizontal or vertically aligned.* **Size** *(b,d) - the region is the smallest if multiple regions are present.* **Contrast** *(c) - the region has the greatest contrast to the surrounding area.* **"Sourroundedness"** *(d) - the region is completely surrounded by another.* **Parallelism** *(e) - the region consists of parallel contours.* **Symmetry** *(f) - symmetrical regions are preferentially perceived as figure, example of 'Rubins vase'.* **Convexity** *(d) - the region is convex.*

differently. This is supported by the work of (Rubin 1921; Rock 1983). Recent work addresses the questions to which degree attention (Kimchi and Peterson 2008) or recognition (Peterson 1994; Vecera and O'Reilly 1998) processes are involved.

Single cell recording Regarding the perception of shape the figure is defined by a contour. Furthermore from psychophysical studies it is known (Peterson 1999) that the region to which the border is assigned is the figure and consequently only one side of contour is viewed as figure.

Such effects can also be measured on a neuronal level, for instance by the border ownership effect (Zhou et al. 2000; Qiu and von der Heydt 2005; Zhaoping 2005; von der Heydt et al. 2005; Sakai and Nishimura 2006; Sugihara et al. 2007) or response enhancements (Lamme 1995; Lamme et al. 1998). For the border ownership effect, neurons were found to encode

2.1. BACKGROUND

the side to which the border belongs. The response enhancement effect occurs for neurons whose receptive field covers the inside of a "figural" region. Whereas the border ownership effect occurs on a very short timescale and can be explained by lateral interaction, whereas the response enhancement effect is supposed to be the results of feedback interaction with neurons of higher level visual areas.

Brain imaging techniques The Lateral Occipital Complex (LOC) in the human brain (Kanwisher et al. 1996; Bar et al. 2001; Grill-Spector et al. 2001; Grill-Spector et al. 2000) is of large interest regarding the processing of object like stimuli since this region is supposed to be a preliminary step for object recognition. The response characteristics of neurons in this area are tuned to object-like shapes, independent of the cue (like motion or texture) that defines the shape and independent of the object identity (Malach et al. 1995). For instance Grill-Spector (2003) found different responses to known and unknown shapes, Similarly object completion effects occur for familiar and unfamiliar objects (Lerner et al. 2002). A different processing of figure and background is supported by Appelbaum, Wade, Vildavski, Pettet, and Norcia (2006). They investigated this visual area with a frequency tagging method to observe figure and background specific responses in the cortex with Electroencephalography (EEG). They found evidences, that indeed the figure and the background are processed very differently or at least distinct cortical networks are involved. According to their results the figure mainly activates the LOC, which is part of the ventral visual pathway. Contrary the background induces responses more dorsally rather than laterally. Furthermore LOC is involved not only in the analysis of shapes but also in its context. Altmann, Deubelius, and Kourtzi (2004) conclude that the processing of context information in LOC is modulated by figure-ground segmentation and grouping processes. In a setup with displays of aligned and oriented Gabor elements (Kovács and Julesz 1993), percepts of global shapes are generated. On this data they analyzed how the fMRI response changes for different shapes and backgrounds. According to their results in LOC, foreground contextual effects are reduced as figure-ground segmentation is allowed by disparity or motions cues. They conclude that figure-ground segmentation seems to be a necessary step to achieve invariance to surrounding clutter.

2.1.2 A system view: The technical role of object segmentation

The concepts outlined before (Sec. 2.1.1) form the basis for computational models of object learning and recognition. These are the distinct visual processing of "what" and "where" as well as hierarchical feed-forward networks (Wersing and Körner 2003; Riesenhuber and Poggio 1999; Mutch and Lowe 2006) to perform a feature extraction that resembles the processing of the ventral visual pathway. The separate processing of the object identity and its location

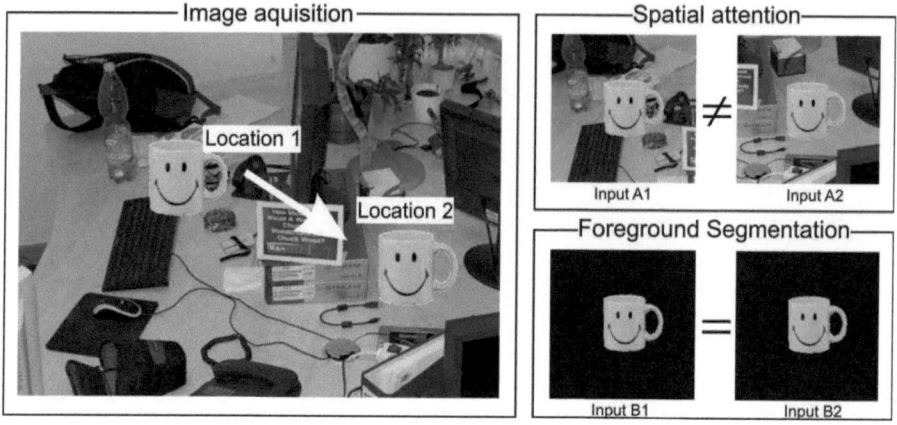

Figure 2.5: *Relation between visual attention and figure-ground segmentation. By means of visual attention different locations in the scene can be determined that are relevant for subsequent feature processing. Around a particular location the object of interest is visible in front of background clutter. In this case a figure-ground segmentation is necessary to focus the feature processing to the relevant image regions.*

in the scene is realized by means of visual saliency and figure-ground segmentation schemes (Fig. 2.5). Recently it was shown that such a biologically motivated feature extraction (Wersing and Körner 2003) in combination with bottom-up attention (Goerick et al. 2005), a rapid segmentation scheme (Steil et al. 2007) and a flexible memory system (Kirstein et al. 2005b) is capable of rapid on-line learning of complex objects in a real-world vision task.

In hierarchical feed-forward networks the figure-ground segmentation is an integral processing step. The feature extraction can be characterized by topographically organized feature detectors that are increasingly specific from one to another layer and invariant to the stimulus variation like scaling, rotation and small local shifts. Each layer in this hierarchy performs some sort of convolution with local features, i.e. applies the same feature detector at all image locations. This is exemplified in Fig. 2.6 (a) by means of four oriented Gabor filters that are used as simple feature detectors in the lowest layer of such hierarchy. The resulting response maps serve as input for the next feature detection layer. Finally an object view can be represented by a high-dimensional feature vector at the highest stage of this hierarchy. In such holistic feature representations the image frame is the reference for coding the position of features. For this reason all features get bound to a certain image location and the feature computation takes place with respect to the whole image. If such feature extraction is applied without a figure-ground segmentation the obtained feature representation includes the properties of the foreground as well as the background. Furthermore it is affected by image transformations of

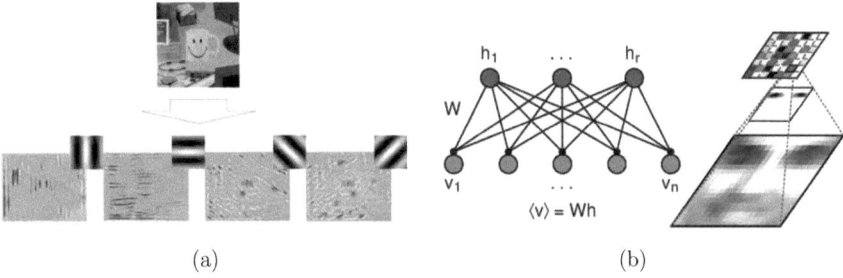

(a)   (b)

Figure 2.6: *Two different types of feature processing. (a) Feature detection by means of convolution, i.e. the application of a feature detector at all image locations. (b) Graph-representation for Non-Negative Matrix Factorization (Lee and Seung 1999). According to this model an image can be composed by a weighted sum of basis vectors, respectively basis images. Each basis image is encoded by a column of the weight matrix W whose contribution is determined by the activation h. Due to the localized activation NMF is regarded as part-based model. However it is holistic in the sense that the image frame serves as reference for the encoding of the visual features.*

the object (e.g. large affine transformations) which changes the feature responses drastically, resulting in poor generalization performance.

From this example we can derive a technical motivation for figure-ground segmentation. In case of a holistic representation like feed-forward hierarchies, all pixel or feature dimensions are equally taken into account, i.e. the object and the background clutter. Independently of the feature extraction stage the dimensionality of the input is important for machine learning techniques because it directly influences the number of training examples. In image processing a very large amount of data would be needed to compensate the large variability of visual data. This is caused by the changing appearance of the object (e.g. by affine/rigid transformation like scale, position, rotation etc.), but also by a dynamically changing and complex structured background. For object recognition in unconstrained interaction scenarios, this leads to a situation where the background and the foreground changes more or less arbitrarily. If the goal is to construct a visual representation for objects, the methods have to generalize over different positions of the object(s) in the scene and different backgrounds. This is not feasible for real-time processing and online-learning so far. The task of figure-ground segmentation is to specify which pixels are relevant for learning to constrain the image analysis and representation of the object region. In this way this preprocessing step separates the object identity from the location in the scene and reduces the complexity of the input data by neglecting the background

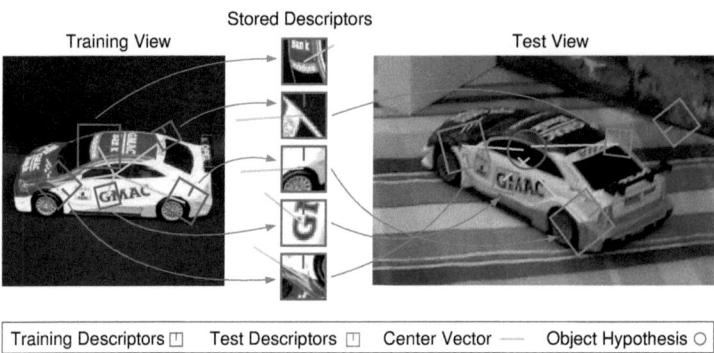

Figure 2.7: *Illustration of a parts-based approach (image taken from (Hasler 2010)). During the training phase a set of representative object features is obtained, which have to be detected in the test views. Dependent on the approach the activation of the features and/or their configuration is important to classify an object view.*

clutter. From a technical viewpoint figure-ground segmentation is relevant to ease the learning and allows a reduction of the necessary amount of training data to teach the system, which is important for the implementation of online-learning.

This argumentation can be applied on alternative models of object learning and recognition. Without a particular focus on biologically plausible models of visual recognition, feature extraction methods like Principle Component Analysis (PCA) or Non-Negative Matrix Factorization (NMF) (Turk and Pentland 1991; Lee and Seung 1999; Liu and Zheng 2004) rely on object segmentation. Those methods base on the assumption that an image can be composed by a weighted sum of "basis" images. The basis can be obtained by taking different optimization criteria into account. In the case of PCA the basis images are the principle components representing the directions of the largest variance of a set of training images. Contrary the optimization of NMF aims for a basis that consists of strict positive basis vectors (Fig. 2.6 (b)). Object learning and recognition takes place on the subspace representation of the input images. If these methods are applied to a whole image it results a global projection, which is affected by foreground as well as background. To avoid this, the methods are applied to individual rigid objects presented in front of uncluttered background. Similar to feed-forward hierarchies subspace methods are sensitive to the object location and affine transformations.

In contrast to the previous examples, parts-based representations rely on the detection of features independently of their position in the image. This methods have to obtain a set of features that are highly distinctive for a particular class, object or views of an object. Such features are distinct parts of the object class like the tires of cars or particular line configurations like the crosses of windows. Parts-based methods can be divided into configurational and combinatorial approaches (Hasler 2010). The configurational approach takes into account the position of the feature in an object-relative manner (i.e. not the image is the reference frame). In (Fergus et al. 2003) objects or categories are represented as collections of features (or parts) and each part has a distinctive appearance and spatial position with respect to object-centered coordinates. Further examples are configurations of Gabor-jets (Loos and von der Malsburg 2002) image patches (Leibe and Schiele 2003) or SIFT descriptors (Lowe 2004). The combinatorial approach (Mel 1997; Ullman et al. 2002; Grauman and Darrell 2007) commonly known as bag-of-features (Csurka et al. 2004; Kinnunen et al. 2009) evaluates only the presence of the features independently of their location. In this approach an image is represented by the vector of maximum activations of the feature in an image.

Those parts-based methods rely on a figure-ground segmentation in the training phase, i.e. for the acquisition of the characteristic parts. To obtain a set of features the algorithms rely on a representative set of training images. From those set the local features, e.g. images patches, and their configuration have to be determined. In principle the amount of information of a single feature is limited, that is, a local feature can be detected on object regions as well as background and only the whole activation profile or configuration is meaningful. A figure-ground segmentation on the training images ensures that the detection of features is only related to object regions. Then, the learning algorithm can concentrate on the relevant activation profiles and configurations. Furthermore in this case the figure-ground segmentation also allows a reduction of the training data.

2.1.3 Summary

In conclusion, figure-ground segmentation focuses the subsequent feature extraction stage on the relevant parts of the scene and allows an efficient construction of object representations. The importance of figure-ground segmentation was exemplified by a biologically motivated object learning architecture. In this model it was shown that a object segmentation stage facilitates the reduction of the number of training samples, increases the learning speed and therefore enables learning in online interactions rather than on offline databases (Steil et al. 2007).

Besides the technical reasons to ease the task for the following processing steps, in this section the question whether this concept is also plausible for biological systems was addressed. Several evidences exist that at some stage in the visual processing the foreground gets separated from the background. Unfortunately it is still unclear at which level figure-ground segmentation can be located and whether it can be interpreted in a technical sense like it is used in computer

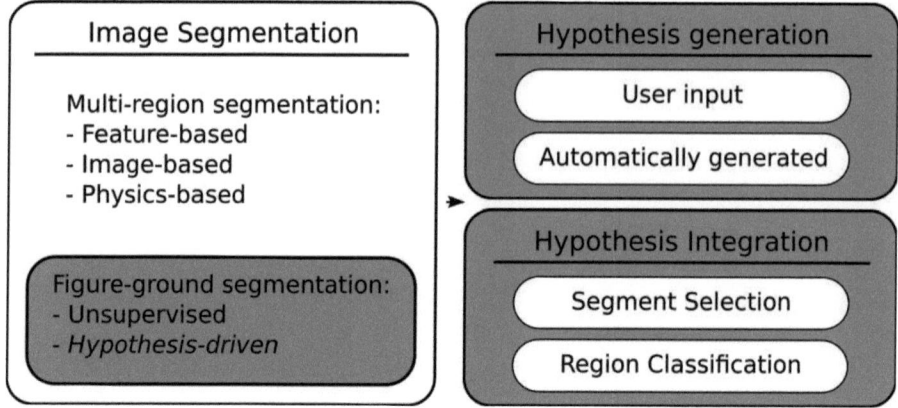

Figure 2.8: *Organization of image segmentation methods: Figure-ground segmentation is a special case of image segmentation. In our work we concentrate on hypothesis-based methods and outline two important aspects, namely the generation and integration of an external segmentation cue.*

vision. Furthermore it is still an open question whether it is a requirement or consequence of the visual processing.

2.2 Computational models

Image segmentation is a basic routine in image analysis and pattern recognition. Due to this fact there is a large amount of literature presenting many different methods to tackle this problem. A comprehensive review can be found in (Vergés Llahí 2005) Chapter 3 and review-papers like (Lucchese and Mitra 2001; Cheng et al. 2001). According to Lucchese and Mitra (2001) segmentation approaches can be grouped by their methodology into feature-based techniques, image-based techniques and physics-based techniques. After a short discussion of this taxonomy, which is necessary to relate the different techniques to each other, the review of the literature organizes the methods in the following way (Fig. 2.8).

The most general concept is unsupervised multi-region segmentation, i.e. the decomposition of an image into several disjoint sub-regions. Those methods can be clearly distinguished from figure-ground segmentation, where only two-region segmentation is performed. The methods for figure-ground segmentation can be separated into unsupervised and hypothesis-driven techniques. While unsupervised techniques aim for a segmentation of the image on the basis of feature similarities, hypothesis-driven methods integrate an external segmentation cue to guide or constrain the segmentation process. Finally several different approaches for hypothesis-based methods are presented where we distinguish them by the source of the external information and how the cue is integrated.

2.2.1 Color image segmentation

Image segmentation aims for a partitioning of an image into disjoint and homogeneous regions that share a common property. By this operation similar parts of the image are grouped together without a relation to the structures in the image or their meaning. As the notion of *similar* is not clearly defined, this problem can be addressed by the usage of different information sources, for instance the homogeneity of regions in their color, texture, coherent motion or depth. The segmentation problem can be formalized in the following way (Lucchese and Mitra 2001; Pal and Pal 1993; Fu and Mui 1981). Given an image $\mathcal{I}$ and a similarity measure D then the segmentation of $\mathcal{I}$ is a partition $\mathcal{P} = \{\mathcal{R}_n | n = 1..N\}$ of $\mathcal{I}$ into a set of N regions $\mathcal{R}_n$, such that[2]:

- $\bigcup_N^1 \mathcal{R}_n = \mathcal{I}$ with $\mathcal{R}_i \cap \mathcal{R}_j \neq \emptyset, \forall i \neq j$
- $D(\mathcal{R}_n) = \text{true } \forall n$
- $D(\mathcal{R}_i \cup \mathcal{R}_j) = \text{false}$ for all adjacent regions R_i and R_j

The first criterion states that the segmentation algorithm obtains a partition of the complete image into a set of non-overlapping regions. The second and third statements formalize the requirement that the elements of a single region are similar to each other whereas a union of two adjacent regions does not fulfill this requirement. In the following the main concepts for different image segmentation techniques are summarized. For a comprehensive overview we refer the interested reader to the related literature (Lucchese and Mitra 2001; Cheng et al. 2001).

Feature-based image segmentation Feature-based techniques rely on the fact that each pixel can be represented by a vector in a particular feature space, e.g. in one of the numerous color spaces. Under the assumption that color is a constant property of a particular surface all pixels related to the same region or surface should have a similar/equal feature vector. Actually in natural environments this is not the case due to the variation of illumination across the surface, the noise of the sensors or the shading effects due to the structure of the surface.

---
[2]Here a separate notation is used, which is not related to the remainder of this thesis (i.e. independent of Sec. A).

Therefore the vectors of the pixels related to distinct parts of the image form a cluster in the used feature space. Approaches based on homogeneity of the features include in particular clustering techniques for example the well known k-means (Lloyd 1982; Macqueen 1967) or the Mean Shift (Comaniciu and Meer 1997) algorithm. Clustering techniques are due to their simplicity one of the most prominent segmentation methods, where the number of clusters corresponds to the number of segments. For the remainder of the thesis clustering techniques are also the most relevant, because they are commonly used for multi-region segmentation as preprocessing step and the succeeding algorithms are applied to the image segments (Hanbury 2008). One extreme of such multi-region segmentation is the concept of super pixels (Ren and Malik 2003), where such super pixels are small compact regions of homogeneous color features. The concept of super-pixels is to process the image on the basis of such small regions instead of pixels to allow for a more efficient processing, larger robustness against noise in the pixel intensities and better representation of the color discontinuities in the image.

Image-based techniques Besides the homogeneity of the region in a specified feature space, for image segmentation the spatial coherence or compactness of the segments is of similar importance. In fact, cluster analysis neglects for the spatial locations of pixels as long as the position of the pixels is not used as features as well. Therefore image-domain-based segmentation techniques address the problem that segments of the image have to be spatially consistent. Classical region-growing and "split & merge" techniques (Lucchese and Mitra 2001) are methods that take the neighborhood of the pixels or the discontinuities in the image into account. Contour-based approaches like active contour models (Kass et al. 1988) or similar level set methods (Osher and Fedkiw 2002) fit a contour-model to the outline of an object and divide the image into the region enclosed by the contour and the outside. The optimization uses a boundary constraint together with a feature-based term. The boundary term ensures that the segmentation yields spatially consistent regions e.g. by restricting the length of the contour or its curvature. The feature-based term reflects the homogeneity of the inside and outside regions. Graph-based models (Boykov and Funka-Lea 2006; Shi and Malik 2000) map the pixels and their similarities onto a graph structure. Algorithms that rely on such graph representation can take these similarities into account to assign a pixel to one of the segments.

Physics-based methods Feature and image-based techniques are often used in combination since different aspects of image segmentation are optimized. While the feature-based techniques form the basis to model the image statistics, the image-based techniques provide additional constraints to derive spatially consistent results. A third group of segmentation algorithm consists of so-called physics-based methods. Here the goal is to compute a large portion of the variability in the image with models of lighting and shading conditions. Large differences in color/feature spaces, which are hard to model by the previous approaches (and cannot be distinguished from structure related variations), can be reduced to a single surface with distinct properties and the given illumination conditions.

Common issues However two principle problems remain that have to be addressed by all methods. The image segmentation problem is basically one of psychophysical perception (Fu and Mui 1981) and not susceptible to a purely analytical solution. Even the segmentation of the same image obtained by several humans will be very different (Martin et al. 2001). As a consequence the segmentation algorithms have to be regarded as domain or problem-specific formulations. Firstly, this addresses the grouping criterion due to a missing general definition of similarity. Secondly the number of segments is task dependent and dependent on the desired "resolution" (e.g. super pixels vs. two-region segmentation), a "true" number does not exist.

Furthermore, a general problem is a missing objective measure for the quality of the segmentation. Therefore different segmentation methods have to be compared with respect to the task they address (Zhang et al. 2008).

2.2.2 Foreground segmentation

2.2.2.1 Unsupervised methods for figure-ground segmentation

Figure-ground segmentation is a special case of image segmentation where the number of regions is restricted to a foreground and a background segment. This does not solve the principle problems but it is an obvious choice in the context of object learning and recognition. At the one hand the methods discussed before can be applied by using only two regions. At the other hand several specialized approaches for figure-ground segmentation have been proposed that can be categorized into unsupervised methods and hypothesis-driven approaches. Two relevant unsupervised methods are the normalized cuts methods (Shi and Malik 2000) and the competitive layer model (Wersing et al. 2001).

Without any initial cue about foreground and background the Normalized Cuts algorithm (Shi and Malik 2000; Ren and Malik 2003) aims for a segmentation of the image into two self-similar regions. The method belongs to spectral graph clustering algorithms and relies on a graph representation of the image. This graph is defined by an interaction matrix computed from all pairwise pixel similarities. The image segmentation is obtained by a partition of the graph into two subsets of nodes (each node corresponds to a pixel) with strong self-similarities but only weak connections to the nodes of the other set. This is formalized by the normalized cut criterion. An approximate solution to cut the graph can be obtained by finding the eigenvector with the second-smallest eigenvalue of a generalized eigenvalue problem.

The Competitive Layer Model has been designed as a dynamic model of Gestalt-based feature binding and segmentation (Wersing et al. 2001). The neural network model consists of multiple layers of topographically structured competitive and cooperative interactions of input features which have to be partitioned into sets of salient groups. The similarities of features are coded by pairwise compatibilities like before. The data-driven learning of these similarity functions has been considered by Weng, Wersing, Steil, and Ritter (2006). To obtain a segmentation of the image an energy function is defined and minimized by neural dynamics.

These unsupervised methods rely on several assumptions. The object has to have a homogeneous appearance (e.g. in color or texture) and its boundaries are clearly defined by high contrast edges that indicate its physical limits. Furthermore one can assume that the image regions that belong to the object are connected to each other, i.e. the physical continuity in case of rigid objects. In unconstrained settings this is not always the case. Objects are heterogeneously colored and can be hardly distinguished from its surrounding background if there is a low contrast to the background. Furthermore occlusions can disrupt their appearance. Regarding online human-robot interaction the methods are also not appropriate for real-time processing on current hardware due to computationally demanding optimization problems.

2.2.2.2 Hypothesis-driven figure-ground segmentation

Unsupervised methods rely on the feature similarities/compatibilities to obtain image segmentation. However in difficult image data the feature-based approach might be insufficient and one cannot expect that an unsupervised algorithm obtains a goal oriented segmentation. Instead of feature similarities, several other cues can provide some additional grouping and shape information (e.g. symmetry, concavity, depth and motion). In the following we assume that an additional cue is available that can provide an initial assignment of image regions to foreground and background. This concept is referred as to hypothesis-driven image segmentation. Where this information comes from and how it is used are two degrees of freedom to characterize the methods published so far. In the following section several methods are presented to obtain an initial hypothesis and we outline the advantages and typical problems. Afterwards two principle ways are discussed how this information is integrated to derive a task oriented segmentation. However, the detailed methodology depends on the particular models and will be explained in more detail in the Chapter 3 and 6. To integrate additional segmentation cues and in particular prior segmentation information was investigated in interactive graphic tools (Rother et al. 2004; Boykov and Jolly 2001), for instance. From user-interaction partial segmentation hints can be obtained and the algorithm has to determine the parts of the image related to the object of interest, respectively consistent with this initial cue. Such image segmentation is necessary to remove a background from an object of interest in order to paste the object in front of a new

2.2. COMPUTATIONAL MODELS

(a) (b) (c)

Figure 2.9: *An illustration of the process of interactive foreground extraction is shown. Together with the image (a) the user has to define a region of interest (b) and/or indicate known portions of the image as foreground or background. This region of interest contains the object and some background clutter. The figure-ground segmentation algorithm has to identify the background clutter in order to obtain a segmentation of the object (c). Dependent on the algorithm the user indication can be used as hard constraint to guide the segmentation process.*

background (Friedland et al. 2007). The information provided by the user is the basis to model the color statistics of both regions (Rother et al. 2004; Unger et al. 2008; Guan and Qiu 2006; Yu and Shi 2004; Blake and Torr 2004; Price et al. 2010). Additionally the user indications can serve as hard constraints for the algorithms if the initial assignments are not allowed to change except explicitly unlabeled regions. Often an interaction between segmentation and foreground indication is used (Rother et al. 2004). The user is able to add further hints if the result is not sufficiently accurate and a refined segmentation is obtained.

In Fig. 2.9 the process of interactive foreground extraction is illustrated. Typically the user has to indicate (see Fig. 2.9) small portions of the image as foreground or background. In the literature this is often referred as scribbles (Bai and Sapiro 2007): small blobs or stripes on the image painted by the user to indicate the assignment of difficult regions. According to Friedland (2006) figure-ground segmentation:

> ... defines foreground to be a set of spatially connected pixels that are "of interest to the user". The rest of the image is considered background. The user has to specify at least a superset of the foreground.

An important problem of such methods is that the information provided by the user often is assumed to be correct. A less constrained scenario can be used if the user provides only a "bounding box" (Fig. 2.9 (b)) for the segmentation where the object is (Lempitsky et al. 2009; Vicente et al. 2009). This small change yields significant consequences in the complexity of the approach. Rather than confident foreground/background assignments now only an outline is available that separates the hypothetical foreground and background without any hard con-

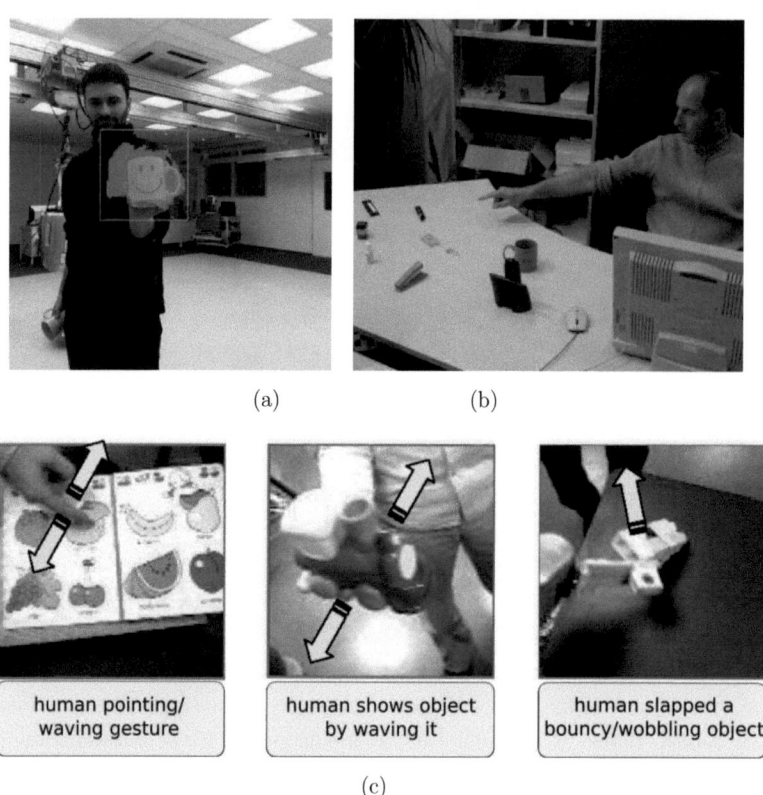

Figure 2.10: *Different examples to obtain an initial segmentation hypothesis. (a) Hypothesis obtained from stereo disparity (Hasler 2010). A region of interest (ROI) that is defined by the "depth blob" contains the object of interest as well as some background. Initially wrong assignments occur at the object boundaries and homogenously colored object regions. (b) Pointing gesture to the location of the object (Bekel et al. 2004). (c) Generation of motion cues (Arsenio 2004b).*

straints. The release of such constraints may complicate the task and reduce the performance, but the advantage is, that the methods are applicable on cues that are not generated by human interaction.

Automatically generated segmentation cues If no user-interaction is available the initial segmentation hypothesis can be automatically generated from external modules. The hypothesis can be obtained from foreground detection (Sun et al. 2006), depth information (Denecke et al. 2009; Steil et al. 2007), saliency (Achanta et al. 2008), motion detection (Fitzpatrick

2003), from statistical priors (Guan and Qiu 2006) or an attention focus (Campbell et al. 2010), among others. Without a direct user-interaction also the detection of skin color can be used to represent the human hint (pointing with the finger) where the object of interest is located in the scene(Arsenio 2004a; Bekel et al. 2004). As a third source of an initial hypothesis this cue can also be generated by an internal representation of known object shapes and parts (Leibe et al. 2007; Yu and Shi 2003; Borenstein et al. 2004; Borenstein and Ullman 2004). A common approach is to model the appearance of an object class or category by a set of representative image patches or more complex structures (Kumar et al. 2005) obtained by a learning algorithm.

Afterwards the parts-based representation is used to detect characteristic patches or features in the target images in order to find/recognize the objects, as well as to segment them from the background. If the goal is the acquisition of a visual representation top-down methods are not appropriate in an initial learning phase since the generation of a hypothesis relies on an already available representation. Furthermore the top-down methods are computationally demanding in the learning phase. For interactive scenarios where real-time and online processing are significant constraints these models are currently not appropriate.

The difference of automatically generated hypothesis to user-provided information is that automatic cues cannot provide confident information about the assignment of each region. A hypothesis is called noisy if its information is partially wrong. For example the user wrongly assigns some portions of the background to foreground. This can be exemplified in Fig. 2.10 (a) - where stereo disparity is used to obtain a region of interest and an initial segmentation of the object in the scene. Because extracting 3D information from 2D images in general is an ill-posed problem, the hypothesis is characterized by a partially inconsistent overlap with the outline/region of the object. The hypothetical segmentation also covers the object only partially on homogenous regions and covers regions of the image that are background. Similar problems occur for motion-based segmentation cues, while other methods e.g. pointing gestures generate only a location rather than an inital segmentation hypothesis.

2.2.2.3 Integrating the hypothesis

To segment an image by means of an initial hypothesis, the methods of the related literature can be distinguished into two methodologies. The first approach bases on the usage of standard algorithms for multi-region image segmentation and a selection mechanism to choose the appropriate segments. The second approach aims for a representation of the feature statistics of the image regions and the successive classification of the pixels.

The first group of methods can be summarized as segment selection models that can be roughly described by four steps. The initial multi-region image segmentation, the generation of the pix-

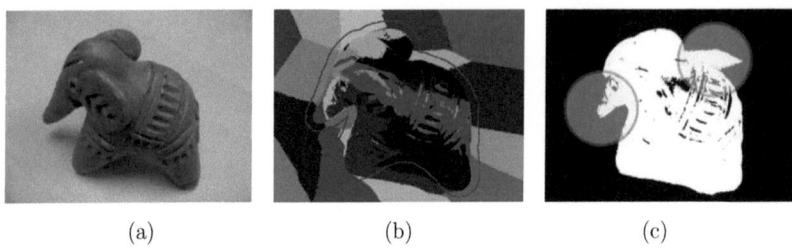

(a) (b) (c)

Figure 2.11: *Illustration of image segmentation by segment selection. A multi-region segmentation like k-means is used to partition of the image (a) into a set of homogenously colored regions (b). In this example the position of the pixels was used as feature as well, resulting in compact segments and the decomposition of the homogenous background region. The hypothesis, indicated by a blue outline, is used to select a subset of segments according to some criterion, e.g. the overlap with the hypothesis (Steil et al. 2007). The final segmentation (c) is determined by the set of selected segments.*

elwise hypothesis, the algorithm to select the appropriate segments according to this hypothesis and a postprocessing to refine the results.

According to the concept of multi-region segmentation the segments should respect the discontinuities in the image more precisely than the hypothesis. In Steil, Götting, Wersing, Körner, and Ritter (2007) a modified k-means algorithm is proposed to segments the image. In a succeeding processing step all segments are selected that show a certain amount of overlap with the hypothesis.

Finally, neighborhood operators are used to enhance the resulting foreground segmentation because the pixelwise clustering is commonly a noisy process. Similar Achanta, Estrada, Wils, and Süsstrunk (2008) uses an initial clustering, a salient region detector to generate the hypothesis and a heuristics to select the matching segments. A method on the basis of the mean shift algorithm was proposed in (Ning et al. 2010). In their work this algorithm is used in combination with a region merging algorithm. The image is segmented using mean shift while the user provides some markers on the image to guide the segmentation process.

The algorithm iteratively merges regions on the basis of their maximum pairwise similarity. The goal is to merge all regions that are not "marked" by the user input with one of the regions that are indicated as foreground or background. They assume that the regions belonging to the object have a higher similarity to the regions indicated as foreground than to the regions indicated as background. Arsenio (2004a) also presents a segment-selection method where the hypothesis is obtained from user-interaction by selectively attending the human actor (hand, arm or finger) by a skin color detection or waving the object. The hypothesis is used as seed

2.2. COMPUTATIONAL MODELS

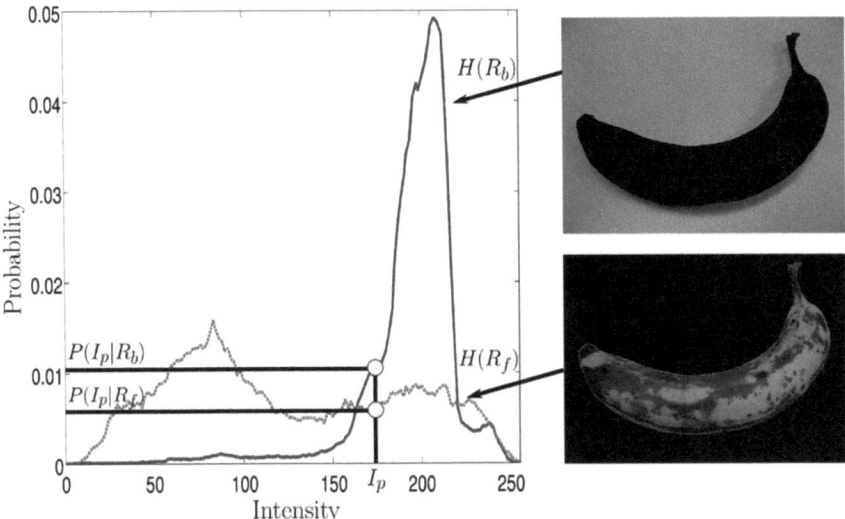

Figure 2.12: *Illustration of the intensity distributions in foreground and background regions. For particular color intensities the probability according to both distributions can be evaluated. By means of the log-likelihood ratio a pixelwise classification of the image can be obtained.*

points for a region growing algorithm to select the segments that are related to the initial cue. The image segmentation is refined by means of an active contour model (Kass et al. 1988) to obtain smooth segmentation boundaries.

In segment selection methods the intelligence of the figure-ground segmentation is shifted to the selection algorithm. This is normally accomplished by means of heuristics that are restricted in their capabilities. Furthermore the representation of the region statistics is independent of the selection mechanism. This is difficult since the multi-region segmentation (e.g. by means of clustering) introduces a model selection problem, that is, if the number of segments is not appropriate several artifacts can occur. If the number of segments is too small the average size of the regions increases. Then the segments may integrate parts of foreground and background near the object boundaries (in particular for similar colors in foreground and background). This results in the selection of background-regions near the object boundary (Fig. 2.11). Contrary, if the number of segments is too high an over-segmentation can occur. Then small segments may be neglected that are not covered by the hypothesis.

Region classification and integration So far several methods about how an initial segmentation hypothesis can be acquired and a first approach to obtain a corresponding figure-ground segmentation were presented. Figure-ground segmentation using the "region classification" approach consists of two basic steps corresponding to the previously mentioned combination of feature-based and image-based segmentation techniques (Sec. 2.2.2):

- (a) the modeling of the feature statistics of the hypothetical foreground and background and

- (b) the consecutive integration of this statistics in energy minimization techniques.

In this section the general concept and methodology of several methods used in the related literature are presented. One possibility to distinguish those methods is to order them by the methodology to model the feature statistics (the first stage). These are histograms, Gaussian Mixtures Models (GMM), kernel density estimation (Bai and Sapiro 2007), prototypical feature representatives i.e. clustering techniques (Friedland 2006) or even using classifiers like Support Vector Machines (SVM) (Duchenne and Audibert 2006; Xu et al. 2008) on the two class problem. For the second stage two prominent energy minimization techniques are graph cuts (Boykov and Jolly 2001; Rother et al. 2004) and level set methods (Osher and Fedkiw 2002). These algorithms allow the integration of further segmentation criteria like neighborhood interactions or additional contour constraints to obtain compact regions and consistent segments regarding the homogeneities and discontinuities in the image.

Here we want to discuss how the information of the hypothesis is used and which particular problems are addressed. A straight forward approach to model color/feature distributions are histograms. For this reason several authors compute histograms of all pixels (respectively the corresponding features) that belong to a certain region. In this case the hypothesis is used to represent the statistics of both regions independently of each other. The classification of each pixel can be obtained by computing the log likelihood ratio. That is, the evaluation of the probability of a pixel to belong to one of the distributions and the classification the pixel according to the largest probability (Fig. 2.12).

Since the pixelwise classification is prone to noise the result can be improved by taking further criteria into account. One possibility is the graph cuts approach that was first proposed by Greig et al. (Greig et al. 1989) in the context of combinatorial optimization for minimizing energy functions. It was applied by Boykov and Jolly (2001) for interactive image segmentation by using cuts on discrete graphs to segment the image (see also Sec. 6.2.2 for a detailed description). The construction of the graphs combines feature-based properties with the topology of the image. Then the min-cut algorithm is used to optimize the partition of the image into two regions with respect to both criteria. The hypothesis is used to compute the region terms that bases on histograms (Boykov and Jolly 2001). Besides the topological aspect and implicit boundary regularization the graph cuts algorithm allows the integration of hard segmentation

2.2. COMPUTATIONAL MODELS

constraints, pixels that are not allowed to change their figure-ground assignment. On the basis of this work, Blake and Torr (2004) propose to model foreground and background regions by Gaussian Mixture Models (GMM). Compared to histograms Gaussian Mixture models can deal more easily with high-dimensional data. This work is further extended in (Rother et al. 2004) towards an "Expectation-Maximization" (EM) optimization procedure where in alternating processing steps the adaptation of the region models and the foreground segmentation is computed. Instead of this EM-style approach a joint optimization of region models and segmentation is addressed by Vicente, Kolmogorov, and Rother (2009). They propose a dual decomposition approach for Markov Random Fields that can also be applied in an iterative procedure. An important restriction of Grab-Cut as well as the Dual Decomposition approach is, that the release of confident user constraints was compensated by the requirement that the initially indicated background regions are fixed, i.e. a hard constraint for the algorithm.

Another possibility to cope with the "bounding box" setting is to impose a topological prior (Lempitsky et al. 2009) rather than only restrict the optimization to a particular region. The color distributions in these methods are represented by Gaussian Mixture Models, where the hypothesis is provided in form of a bounding box. The additional prior prevents the solution from excessive shrinking by constraining the result to a solution where the segmentation have parts that are sufficiently close to each of the sides of the bounding box. This requires that the "users provide bounding boxes that are not too loose, but sufficiently tight". For the optimization a new approximate graph cut-based algorithm called pinpointing (Lempitsky et al. 2009) is used.

An interesting alternative to statistical region modeling was proposed in (Duchenne and Audibert 2006). In this work a classification of the pixels (i.e. features) is performed using a Support Vector Machine for the purpose of figure-ground segmentation. This supervised classification approach relies on the correctness of the training data, respectively their labels. Similar to the likelihood from feature distributions the classification of the pixels finally can be integrated in the graph cuts optimization as well. In contrast to this work, Xu, Chen, and Huang (2008) introduce robustness to the noise in the hypothesis by an ensemble-based learning approach. That is, separate Support Vector Machines are trained with random subsets of the available data. The outputs of the SVM classifiers are combined by majority voting assuming that the errors of the separate SVMs are uncorrelated.

This review concentrates so far on the graph cuts approach and its extensions. Alternatively level set methods are a second prominent energy minimization technique. Here the segmentation problem is addressed in the context of implicit variational methods for contour optimization (Boykov and Funka-Lea 2006). The overall methodology is similar to the iterative graph cuts discussed before. The level set formalism also allows to integrate the information of region models, e.g. from histograms (Li and Xiao 2009; Weiler and Eggert 2007) into an optimization where additional constraints are imposed. The level set formulation includes an additional smoothness term (e.g. penalizing the length of the contour) to derive compact foreground segmentations. Compared to graph cuts the initial region assignment of the hypothesis can be used to initialize the region models but also the level set function itself. From this initial value the level set function iteratively evolved by means of a partial differential equation. Both methods are discussed in more detail in Chapter 6.

2.2.2.4 Open issues

To summarize this section we discuss two problems that are only partially reflected in the state-of-the-art. The goal of all presented methods is to obtain an image segmentation that is consistent with an initial segmentation cue. The algorithms take into account the statistics of the data and the external information, e.g. the color statistics of the regions, the region indication provided by a user and prior assumptions that are integrated into the algorithm itself. Many of those methods are designed for interactive image segmentation where a user can provide confident segmentation cues. This information can be exploited to obtain a classification for the unlabeled pixels. Often the user indication is assumed to be correct and used as hard segmentation constraints for the algorithm. If this requirement is released a less constrained user-interaction and the application with respect to automatically generated segmentation cues are possible. Then the methods can be judged by their robustness against partially wrong segmentation hypotheses and the missing hard segmentation constraints. So far if a bounding box is used at the same moment also the constraint that the initial background assignment is fixed, is introduced (Vicente et al. 2009; Rother et al. 2004; Lempitsky et al. 2009). This assumption is correct as long as the initial segmentation cue is a superset of all foreground pixels in the image. If the object is only partially covered, then such methods are not capable to obtain a segmentation that completes the missing information. To our knowledge so far only one model directly addresses the noise in the hypothesis. In the work of Xu, Chen, and Huang (2008) an ensemble-based region classification on the basis of Support Vector Machines was proposed. A further problem is the occurrence of same colors in foreground and background since the statistical or descriptive modeling of foreground and background depends on the underlying feature space. If histograms and Gaussian Mixture Models are used the representation of the region statistics is independent for each region and the discriminability of the features is not taken into account.

2.3 Discussion

In this chapter we discussed the problem of figure-ground segmentation and its origins. Figure-ground segmentation addresses the grouping of pixels into multiple spatially coherent regions according to a specified similarity function on some feature space. Compared to multi-region image segmentation in figure-ground segmentation the image is decomposed into only two regions, containing the object of interest and the remaining background. From the related literature we presented several methods that concentrated on figure-ground segmentation. One dominant application of these methods is in interactive graphics tools to remove the background from an object of interest by means of user-interaction. Besides several reasons that motivate the necessity of such mechanism in a technical way we also motivated its important role in the biological counterpart. Inspired by the knowledge about visual processing in the human brain it is an important step to separate the processing of the object data from the location in the scene/image. Therefore a figure-ground segmentation is a necessary component to build-up complex visual learning and recognition architectures.

In the remaining work of this thesis we will concentrate on figure-ground segmentation in the context of online visual learning. Unfortunately the methods from interactive segmentation tools cannot be directly transferred to this scenario. One reason is the requirement of a confident figure-ground hypothesis in the form of scribbles. This information is assumed to be correct and used to adapt the region models, which are used in turn to classify the remaining pixels. Methods that release such constraints still rely on hard constraints e.g. the initial background region cannot be changed. If such concept is used on automatically determined cues, the segmentation may fail due to the fact that the external cue does not completely cover the object. However we conclude that the hypothesis-based figure-ground segmentation scheme is the most appropriate for our intended scenario. For this reason we impose two requirements for a figure-ground segmentation scheme. The methods have to obtain a solution that is consistent with the hypothesis as well as the image data. With respect to an automatic application the method should also be capable to segment objects without any use of confident information or hard constraints. The model has to cope with a noisy hypothesis that can include wrong labels. A second requirement is the weighting of the image features in order to discriminate between foreground and background. This capability is important to cope with similar colors in foreground and background. In interactive graphics tools this problem is not as relevant since the user can compensate it by means of hard segmentation constraints. Without this additional information the methods have to solve this problem by an automatic feature weighting.

Chapter 3
A learning vector quantization approach

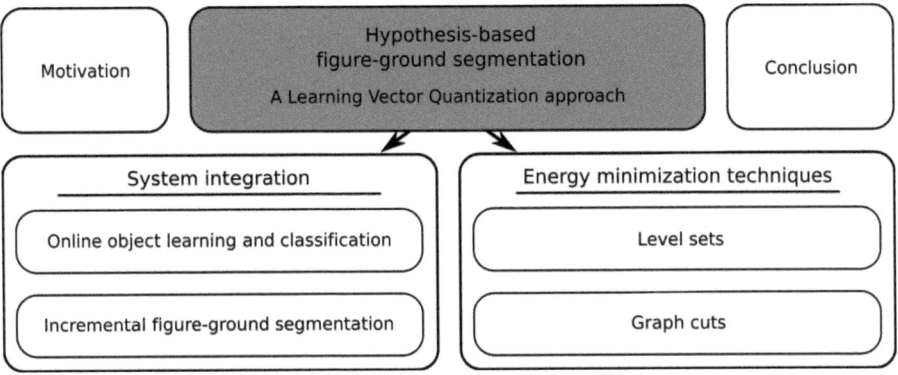

In Chapter 2 the concept of hypothesis-based figure-ground segmentation was introduced. According to this concept, machine learning techniques are applied to the image data together with an initial segmentation in order to obtain a pixelwise classification of an image. Two relevant problems for this procedure are to achieve robustness against partially wrong (noisy) hypotheses and to respect the discriminability of the image features in order to distinguish between foreground and background. In related work those problems are addressed by separate models using ensemble-based learning or feature weighting techniques (Xu et al. 2008; Wang 2007), for instance. In this chapter we present a Learning Vector Quantization approach that can be applied for this task and can deal with both problems simultaneously (Denecke et al. 2008; Denecke et al. 2009). In comparison to the related literature the emphasis of the method is not the best possible segmentation rather than the robustness under real world conditions without confident user-interaction. The chapter starts with a description of the Learning Vector Quantization algorithm and its extensions. Afterwards we will present the methodology to apply this algorithm to the figure-ground segmentation problem. In the second part of this chapter the properties of the model are analyzed and several evaluations are presented.

3.1 Introduction

Learning vector quantization is a supervised learning algorithm to construct a prototype-based classifier for a set of labeled data points in a multidimensional feature space (Kohonen et al. 2001). Originally three different heuristics were proposed (LVQ1, LVQ2.1, and LVQ3) to adapt the set of prototypical feature representatives by means of competitive adaptation of the prototypes of distinct classes. These algorithms are attractive due to several reasons. Like any prototype-based model (e.g. k-means Sec. 2.2.2.1) the underlying structure is transparent and depends on few model parameters. Therefore it is easy to analyze the behavior of the algorithm and interpret the results. It can naturally deal with multi-class problems and can be used to model complex feature distributions of the classes as long as the number of representatives is large enough. For this algorithm exists a rich repertoire of applications and extension (see (Schneider et al. 2009a) for an overview of related work). The Generalized Learning Vector Quantization (GLVQ) algorithm was introduced by Sato and Yamada (1995) that replaces the LVQ2.1 learning heuristic by stochastic gradient descent on a well defined cost function. However, the overall model structure is similar to the original LVQ algorithm.

3.2 Generalized Learning Vector Quantization

The algorithm requires a dataset $\mathcal{D} := \{\vec{\xi} \mid \vec{\xi}(\mathbf{x}) \in \mathbb{R}^M\}$ of real-valued feature vectors. To each of the data points a label $c[\vec{\xi}] \in \mathbb{N}$ is assigned, where $c[\cdot]$ is regarded as a property of the feature vector rather than a function. In anticipation of the intended application of the method, the data points are indexed by $\mathbf{x} \in \Omega$ that refers to the location in the image plane Ω. The GLVQ algorithm bases on a network of N class-specific prototypical feature representatives $\mathcal{P} := \{\vec{w}_p \in \mathbb{R}^M \mid p = 1..N\}$, shortly referred to as prototypes. Due to the supervised learning setting the prototypes are also labeled, which is indicated by $c[\vec{w}_p] \in \{0, 1\}$. For figure-ground segmentation a two class setup is used and the label encodes the a priori (e.g. by the user) assigned class-membership of each prototype. One common method to initialize the prototypes of the network is to draw random samples $\vec{\xi} \in \mathcal{D}$ from the data distribution and take the feature vectors as initial representative for each class. Afterwards the GLVQ learning dynamics optimizes the representatives $\vec{w}_p$ in such a way that the following cost function is minimized:

3.2. GENERALIZED LEARNING VECTOR QUANTIZATION

$$E_{\text{glvq}}[\mathcal{P},\mathcal{D}] := \sum_{\vec{\xi}(\mathbf{x})} \sigma\left(\mu(\mathcal{P},\vec{\xi}(\mathbf{x}))\right), \text{ with } \sigma(x) = \frac{1}{1+e^{-x}} \quad (3.1)$$

$$\mu(\mathcal{P},\vec{\xi}(\mathbf{x})) = \frac{d_J - d_K}{d_J + d_K} \quad (3.2)$$

Here the variables $d_J = d(\vec{\xi}(\mathbf{x}), \vec{w}_J)$ and $d_K = d(\vec{\xi}(\mathbf{x}), \vec{w}_K)$ are the distances of a feature vector $\vec{\xi} \in \mathcal{D}$ to the most similar prototype $\vec{w}_J$, $c[\vec{\xi}] = c[\vec{w}_J]$ of the correct class and $\vec{w}_K$ of an incorrect class, respectively. The distance measure $d(\cdot)$ is usually the Euclidean metrics $d(\vec{\xi}, \vec{w}) = \|\vec{\xi} - \vec{w}\|$ or the squared Euclidean metrics $d(\vec{\xi}, \vec{w}) = (\vec{\xi} - \vec{w})^T (\vec{\xi} - \vec{w})$. Compared to the standard LVQ algorithms (Kohonen et al. 2001) this optimization takes place by means of stochastic gradient descent on randomly chosen data samples $(\vec{\xi}(\mathbf{x}), c[\vec{\xi}])$. In the case of the squared Euclidean metrics for each data sample the two best matching prototypes $\vec{w}_J$ and $\vec{w}_K$ are adapted as follows:

$$\begin{aligned}\vec{w}_J &= \vec{w}_J - \alpha \cdot \phi' \cdot \mu^+(\mathcal{P},\vec{\xi}) \cdot \frac{\partial d_J}{\partial \vec{w}_J}, \\ \vec{w}_K &= \vec{w}_K + \alpha \cdot \phi' \cdot \mu^-(\mathcal{P},\vec{\xi}) \cdot \frac{\partial d_K}{\partial \vec{w}_K}\end{aligned} \quad (3.3)$$

with

$$\begin{aligned}\mu^+(\mathcal{P},\vec{\xi}) &= \frac{2d_K}{(d_J+d_K)^2}, \\ \mu^-(\mathcal{P},\vec{\xi}) &= \frac{2d_J}{(d_J+d_K)^2}\end{aligned} \quad (3.4)$$

and

$$\phi' = \frac{d_J - d_K}{d_J + d_K} \quad (3.5)$$

and the derivative of the squared Euclidean metric

$$\frac{\partial d(\vec{\xi} - \vec{w})}{\partial \vec{w}} = -2(\vec{\xi} - \vec{w}) \quad (3.6)$$

The gradient descent is iterated until the model converges. The classification of data samples follows a simple "winner takes all" scheme. A sample $\vec{\xi}$ is classified by its best matching prototype, i.e. it is mapped to the class $c[\vec{\xi}] = c[\vec{w}_i]$ with $d(\vec{\xi}, \vec{w}_i) < d(\vec{\xi}, \vec{w}_j) \forall j \neq i$. The model depends only on two parameters that have to be specified beforehand, the learning rate α and the number of prototypes N.

Large margin classification The optimization of the cost function (Eq. 3.1) affects two aspects. The first aspect is the minimization of the classification error. A negative numerator in Eq. 3.2 indicates a correct classification. In this case the distance to the wrong class is larger than to a prototype of the correct class. The second aspect is the maximization of the margin $\mu(\mathcal{P}, \vec{\xi}(\mathbf{x})) = (d_J - d_K)/(d_J + d_K), \mu(\mathcal{P}, \vec{\xi}(\mathbf{x})) \in [-1, 1]$ between both distances d_J and d_K. In other words, the optimization aims for a large difference between the best matching prototypes of the correct class and those of the incorrect classes (Schneider et al. 2009a; Crammer et al. 2002). The margin is in particular important since this value can be regarded as the confidence of the classification. Furthermore this term is important with respect to the generalization ability. The goal of learning is not only to achieve a small classification error on the training data but also to achieve a good generalization performance to previously unseen data-points. That is, the algorithm has to find a model for the data that represents the underlying regularities or structures of the dataset. As pointed out by Biehl, Hammer, Schneider, and Villmann (2009) LVQ networks exhibit a large robustness towards over-fitting. In this work they showed that similar to SVMs the generalization ability of LVQ classifiers is independent of the input dimensionality. Instead of the input dimensionality the margin is the relevant quantity for characterizing this ability. Therefore they argue that LVQ classifiers can be interpreted as large margin classifiers similar to SVM.

3.2.1 Adaptive metrics in GLVQ

Similarity-based clustering and classification depends on the underlying metrics and the used feature space. In general, we cannot expect that all feature dimensions are equally important for the classification. Furthermore different weightings of the dimensions have a strong impact on the success of such methods if the Euclidean metrics is used. The choice of the Euclidean metrics bases on the assumption of isotropic clusters. To take care of different scales in the data or relevance for the classification the data has to be preprocessed. If this is not possible beforehand the metrics have to be flexible enough to respect different scalings in the data, the relevance for the classification, or even correlations between several features. Since the choice of the Eulicdean metrics as similarity measure is often too strict, several alternative methods were proposed in order to allow a flexible weighting of the feature dimensions.

One of the most popular metrics manipulations is the introduction of feature-specific weighting factors to compensate for different scales of the feature dimensions. The Adaptive Scene-Dependent Filter (ASDF) (Steil et al. 2007) approach globally modifies the metrics by a rescaling of the features-channels with their variance and a feature-specific a priori weighting factor. However, determining the appropriate weightings in an automatic fashion is an important problem. Recently, for Learning Vector Quantization it has been proposed to optimize

3.2. GENERALIZED LEARNING VECTOR QUANTIZATION

Method	Metrics $d(\vec{\xi}, \vec{w}_p)$
GLVQ ($\mathcal{Q}$)	$\sum_i^M (\xi_i - w_i)^2$
GRLVQ ($\mathcal{Q}_V^G$)	$\sum_i^M \lambda_i (\xi_i - w_i)^2$
GMLVQ ($\mathcal{Q}_M^G$)	$(\vec{\xi} - \vec{w}_p)^T \Lambda (\vec{\xi} - \vec{w}_p)$
LGRLVQ ($\mathcal{Q}_V^L$)	$\sum_i^M \lambda_i^p (\xi_i - w_i)^2$
LGMLVQ ($\mathcal{Q}_M^L$)	$(\vec{\xi} - \vec{w}_p)^T \Lambda_p (\vec{\xi} - \vec{w}_p)$

Table 3.1: *Overview of the different metric adaptation schemes for Generalized Learning Vector Quantization.*

such factors for the classification problem at hand. Based on the Generalized LVQ method, Hammer and Villmann (2002) have extended the standard Euclidean metrics by introducing a global relevance-factor for each feature dimension (Generalized Relevance LVQ (GRLVQ)). This leads to the squared weighted Euclidean metrics:

$$d(\vec{\xi}, \vec{w}) = \|\vec{\xi} - \vec{w}\|_\lambda^2 = \sum_i^M \lambda_i (\xi_i - w_i)^2, \tag{3.7}$$

where $\lambda_i \geq 0$ and $\sum_{i=1}^M \lambda_i = 1$. In further investigations, the following two extensions of this concept have been proposed (Schneider et al. 2009a; Schneider et al. 2009b). Firstly, using an $M \times M$ matrix of relevance-factors (Generalized Matrix LVQ, GMLVQ results in the metrics

$$d(\vec{\xi}, \vec{w}) = (\vec{\xi} - \vec{w})^T \Lambda (\vec{\xi} - \vec{w}). \tag{3.8}$$

Since the relevance matrices Λ have to be positive semi-definite to yield valid metrics, i.e. $d(\vec{\xi}, \vec{w}) = (\vec{\xi} - \vec{w})^T \tilde{\Lambda} \tilde{\Lambda}^T (\vec{\xi} - \vec{w}) = (\tilde{\Lambda}^T (\vec{\xi} - \vec{w}))^2 \geq 0$, it is necessary to adapt $\tilde{\Lambda}$, where $\Lambda = \tilde{\Lambda} \tilde{\Lambda}^T$. Additionally, the diagonal elements are normalized by $\sum_{i=1}^M \Lambda_{i,i} = 1$ to stabilize the algorithm.

The second extension introduces local relevance-vectors/matrices $\vec{\lambda}_p, \Lambda_p$ specific for each prototype, called localized GMLVQ/GRLVQ (LGMLVQ/LGRLVQ) to allow prototype specific metrics manipulations, i.e. $d(\vec{\xi}, \vec{w}_p) = (\vec{\xi} - \vec{w}_p)^T \Lambda_p (\vec{\xi} - \vec{w}_p)$. In particular this modification affects the class of decision boundaries that can be obtained by the model. In the case of the Euclidean metrics non-linear decision boundaries are possible by increasing the number of prototypes. But the decision boundaries are restricted to piecewise linear ones, characterized by a hyperplane between each pair of prototypes. The kernelized distance computation introduces non-linear decision boundaries also for the case of only one prototype for each class and even more complex ones if multiple prototypes are used (Fig. 3.3). As described by Crammer, Gilad-Bachrach, Navot, and Tishby (2002) a reduced number of prototypes is possible while a similar performance to standard LVQ with multiple prototypes can be achieved. Since the computational effort of the model depends on the number of prototypes this property is an advantage compared to standard LVQ learning.

While the metrics is changed, the overall error function and its optimization is kept for the advanced LVQ schemes. Stochastic gradient descent is used to minimize the error defined by Eq. 3.1 on randomly chosen pairs $(\vec{\xi}, c[\vec{\xi}])$. In each iteration, the two best matching prototypes $\vec{w}_J$ and $\vec{w}_K$ and the corresponding relevance-factors Λ_J and Λ_K are updated according to $\vec{w} \leftarrow \vec{w} - \alpha \cdot \partial E/\partial \vec{w}$, $\Lambda \leftarrow \Lambda - \beta \cdot \partial E/\partial \Lambda$. See (Schneider et al. 2009a) for a comprehensive overview of the update formulas. For the most complex case, LGMLVQ, the network is adapted by means of:

$$\Delta \vec{w}_J = \frac{\partial E}{\partial \vec{w}_J} = \frac{\partial \sigma}{\partial \mu} \frac{\partial \mu}{\partial d_J} \frac{\partial d_J}{\partial \vec{w}_J} = -\alpha \cdot \frac{e^{-\mu}}{(1+e^{-\mu})^2} \frac{2 d_K}{(d_J + d_K)^2} (-2 \tilde{\Lambda} \tilde{\Lambda}^T (\vec{\xi} - \vec{w})),$$

$$\Delta \vec{w}_K = \frac{\partial E}{\partial \vec{w}_K} = \frac{\partial \sigma}{\partial \mu} \frac{\partial \mu}{\partial d_K} \frac{\partial d_K}{\partial \vec{w}_K} = \alpha \cdot \frac{e^{-\mu}}{(1+e^{-\mu})^2} \frac{2 d_J}{(d_J + d_K)^2} (-2 \tilde{\Lambda} \tilde{\Lambda}^T (\vec{\xi} - \vec{w})),$$

$$\Delta \tilde{\Lambda}_J = \frac{\partial E}{\partial \tilde{\Lambda}_J} = \frac{\partial \sigma}{\partial \mu} \frac{\partial \mu}{\partial d_J} \frac{\partial d_J}{\partial \tilde{\Lambda}_J} = -\beta \cdot \frac{e^{-\mu}}{(1+e^{-\mu})^2} \frac{2 d_K}{(d_J + d_K)^2} \cdot (M_J^T + M_J), \quad (3.9)$$

$$\Delta \tilde{\Lambda}_K = \frac{\partial E}{\partial \tilde{\Lambda}_K} = \frac{\partial \sigma}{\partial \mu} \frac{\partial \mu}{\partial d_K} \frac{\partial d_K}{\partial \tilde{\Lambda}_K} = \beta \cdot \frac{e^{-\mu}}{(1+e^{-\mu})^2} \frac{2 d_J}{(d_J + d_K)^2} \cdot (M_K^T + M_K),$$

$$M_J = \tilde{\Lambda}(\vec{\xi} - \vec{w}_J) \cdot (\vec{\xi} - \vec{w}_J)^T,$$

$$M_K = \tilde{\Lambda}(\vec{\xi} - \vec{w}_K) \cdot (\vec{\xi} - \vec{w}_K)^T.$$

To keep a compact notation, we will in the following refer to the Generalized Vector Quantization with the symbol $\mathcal{Q}$ and use the indices L, G for localized or global metrics extension and M, V for the relevance matrices Λ or vectors $\vec{\lambda}$ (Tab. 3.1). That is, GLVQ=$\mathcal{Q}$, GRLVQ=$\mathcal{Q}_V^G$, GMLVQ=$\mathcal{Q}_M^G$, LGRLVQ=$\mathcal{Q}_V^L$, LGMLVQ=$\mathcal{Q}_M^L$.

3.3 Application of GLVQ for image segmentation

As pointed out in Chapter 2, hypothesis-based figure-ground segmentation methods are applied in interactive image segmentation, where the user has to provide some constraints by indicating which regions belong to foreground or background respectively. A less constrained scenario is the usage of a bounding box as initial segmentation cue (Sec. 2.2.2). This capability allows the automatic application of the method without confident prior information about the hypothetical region assignment. The goal of the algorithm is to identify and neglect the background pixels that were wrongly included in the hypothesis (Fig. 3.1 (c)) and to obtain a segmentation of the object of interest. However the usage of a bounding box implies several difficulties for state-

3.3. APPLICATION OF GLVQ FOR IMAGE SEGMENTATION

(a) (b) (c) (d)

Figure 3.1: *Typical problem setting: the user provides an input image (a) together with an initial segmentation hypothesis $\mathcal{H}$ (b), in this case a bounding box. The algorithm has to determine a segmentation $\mathcal{A}$ that is as close as possible to the object of interest. In this example the desired result (c) is emphasized by the green color while the wrongly included background pixels are emphasized in red. For evaluation also a ground truth segmentation $\mathcal{A}^*$ is available on some of the datasets (d).*

of-the-art methods (Sec. 2.2.2.4). For our approach a classifier for foreground and background separation is trained with GLVQ where we can show that this method can directly deal with those problems. This method uses prototypical feature representatives to model both regions on the basis of the initial hypothesis that is used as supervised label of the image data. According to the application of this method for figure-ground segmentation, we want to define our target as the separation of the image data into two classes that can be well distinguished in the feature space and form a spatially consistent region in the image domain.

The input data consist of a stack of M topographically ordered feature maps $\mathcal{F} := \{F_i | i = 1..M\}$, where in the simplest case the three RGB color channels can be used. The choice of these features is not constrained to a particular color space and the concepts can be generalized to an arbitrary number of feature maps, e.g. containing information about texture (Duchenne et al. 2008; Wang 2007). In this work the RGB color-space is used together with the pixel position $(F_1(\mathbf{x}) = R(\mathbf{x}), F_2(\mathbf{x}) = G(\mathbf{x}), F_3(\mathbf{x}) = B(\mathbf{x}), F_4(\mathbf{x}) = x, F_5(\mathbf{x}) = y)$, where $\mathbf{x} = \{x, y\}$ stands for the position of the pixel in the image plane Ω. The pixel coordinates (x, y) are important as additional features for an implicit region modeling (Xu et al. 2008; Bai et al. 2009). In order to apply numerical methods, the stack of maps $\mathcal{F}$ is represented by a set of vectors $\vec{\xi} \in \mathbb{R}^M$, where each pixel defines a feature vector. In other words, these feature maps can be represented as dataset $\mathcal{D} := \{\vec{\xi}(\mathbf{x}) = (F_1(\mathbf{x})..F_M(\mathbf{x}))^T | \mathbf{x} \in \Omega\}$. In the following two different notations are used dependent on the context, where $\vec{\xi} \in \mathcal{D}$ is equivalent to the notation $\vec{\xi}(\mathbf{x}), \mathbf{x} \in \Omega$.

Besides the input image (Fig. 3.1 (a)), a further requirement is an initial segmentation hypothesis $\mathcal{H}$ (Fig. 3.1 (b)) that provides a label $c[\vec{\xi}] \in \mathbb{N}$ for each pixel (i.e. its corresponding feature vector). In our scenario this information is only partially reliable, i.e. such hypotheses may contain of wrong feature labeling. This is an important problem if a bounding box is used (see Fig. 3.1 (c)), but can also occur in interactive image segmentation when the user accidentally assigns some image regions to the wrong class. If the segmentation cue is obtained via computational models a reliable segmentation hypothesis cannot be guaranteed. Therefore, generalizing to the relevant object parts from this hypothesis and discarding the background is complicated. This is caused by partially overlapping feature-clusters due to the noisy hypothesis, as well as by similar features (i.e. colors) in regions of the object and background.

3.3.1 Algorithm

To apply the GLVQ algorithm for image segmentation the concept of the hypothesis is used in the following way. We state the task of object segmentation as a binary classification problem and use Generalized Learning Vector Quantization to adapt a classifier for the pixels. The hypothesis $\mathcal{H}$ is represented as a binary map indicating which pixels belong to foreground $\mathcal{H}(\mathbf{x}) = 1$ or background $\mathcal{H}(\mathbf{x}) = 0$. This hypothesis $\mathcal{H}$ is used as label $c[\vec{\xi}(\mathbf{x})] := \mathcal{H}(\mathbf{x})$ for the image features to adapt a codebook of N class-specific prototypes $\mathcal{P} := \{\vec{w}_p \in \mathbb{R}^M | p = 1..N\}$. The clusters in the data $\mathcal{F}$ (homogeneous regions in the image) are represented by the prototypes $\vec{w}_p$. For figure-ground segmentation a setup with two classes is used where $c[\vec{w}_p] \in \{0, 1\}$ encodes the class-membership, assigned by the user, of each prototype to figure or ground. The codebook $\mathcal{P}$ is initialized for each class separately with a random sampling of features $\vec{\xi}$ from the first image (respectively $\mathcal{F}, \mathcal{H}$). To obtain a segmentation $\mathcal{A}$ of an image on the basis of the adapted classifier, all feature vectors $\vec{\xi}(\mathbf{x})$ (i.e. pixels of a particular frame) are mapped to the label of the prototype $\vec{w}_p$ with the smallest distance $d(\vec{\xi}(\mathbf{x}), \vec{w}_p)$. The general concept for hypothesis-based image segmentation using this method can be summarized with the following pseudo code:

1 Input: feature maps $\mathcal{F}$ and hypothesis $\mathcal{H}$

2 Preprocessing of feature maps if necessary:
$F_i \leftarrow T_F(F_i)$

3 Preprocessing of hypothesis if necessary (e.g. binarization):
$\mathcal{H} \leftarrow T_H(\mathcal{H})$

4 Initialization of codebook $\mathcal{P} = \{\vec{w}_p\}, p = 1,.., N$ if not already done

5 Adaptation (for t update steps)

3.3. APPLICATION OF GLVQ FOR IMAGE SEGMENTATION

- Select $\vec{\xi}(\mathbf{x})$ at random position $\mathbf{x} \in \Omega$

- Find best matching prototypes $\vec{w}_J$ for the correct label, $\vec{w}_K$ for the incorrect label

$$\vec{w}_J = \{\vec{w}_p \in \mathcal{P} | d(\vec{w}_p, \vec{\xi}(\mathbf{x})) = \min_{q, c[\vec{w}_q] = \mathcal{H}(\mathbf{x})} d(\vec{w}_q, \vec{\xi}(\mathbf{x}))\}$$

$$\vec{w}_K = \{\vec{w}_p \in \mathcal{P} | d(\vec{w}_p, \vec{\xi}(\mathbf{x})) = \min_{q, c[\vec{w}_q] \neq \mathcal{H}(\mathbf{x})} d(\vec{w}_q, \vec{\xi}(\mathbf{x}))\}$$

- Update prototypes with learning rate α

  $\vec{w}_J \leftarrow \vec{w}_J - \alpha \cdot \partial E / \partial \vec{w}_J$ (attract the prototype of the correct class)

  $\vec{w}_K \leftarrow \vec{w}_K - \alpha \cdot \partial E / \partial \vec{w}_K$ (push away the prototype of the incorrect class)

- Update relevance factors according to the choice of the metrics $d(\cdot, \cdot)$, see Sec. 3.2.1

6 Determine foreground segmentation by means of nearest neighbor classification

$$\mathcal{A}(\mathbf{x}) = c[\vec{w}_p], d(\vec{\xi}(\mathbf{x}), \vec{w}_p) < d(\vec{\xi}(\mathbf{x}), \vec{w}_r), \forall r \neq p, \{r, p\} \in \mathcal{P}$$

Related work With respect to the related work outlined in Chapter 2 this approach can be regarded as feature-based technique (Sec. 2.2.1). Here the feature distributions of foreground and background are modeled with prototypical feature representatives. The model itself is adapted by means of supervised learning according to the hypothesis $\mathcal{H}$. Therefore the integration of the hypothesis follows the region modeling technique (Sec. 2.2.2.3).

A similar approach on the basis of the segment-selection techniques was presented in (Steil et al. 2007). The ASDF model (Steil et al. 2007), differs in three aspects from the proposed method. In their more heuristically setting, Steil et al. considered an unsupervised clustering approach and therefore only w_J is adapted in step 5 where $c[\vec{w}_p] = 1, \forall p \in \mathcal{P}$, is equal for all prototypes. After adapting the prototypes, the foreground segmentation (step 6) is constructed with a heuristics to determine a subset of prototypes. The criterion for this selection bases on the overlap of the corresponding segment with the initial hypothesis $\mathcal{H}$. Additionally to the original hypothesis derived from depth and skin color information a further position prior, in form of an image centered circular map is used. The most important difference concerns the distance computation, which is Euclidean and not adapted during learning. Instead the ASDF approach globally modifies the metrics in a preprocessing step by a rescaling of the features maps $\bar{\xi}_j := f_i \cdot (\xi_j / \sigma_i^2)$ with their variance σ_i^2 of the feature channel and a feature-specific a priori weighting factor f_i.

3.3.2 Relevant properties of the model

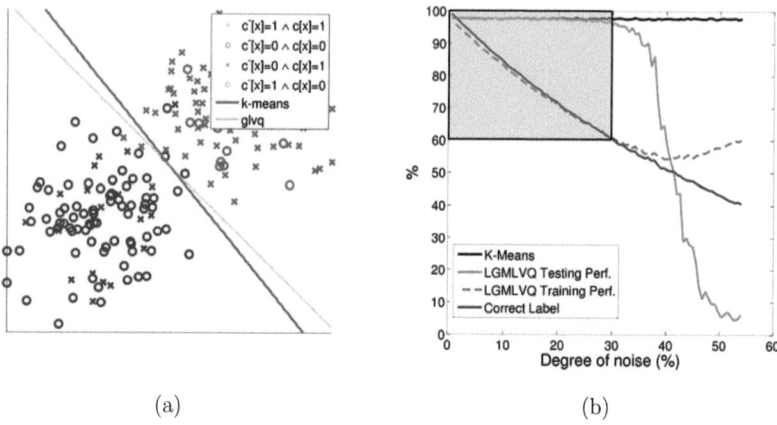

(a) (b)

Figure 3.2: *Example of the noisy supervised information on two-dimensional artificial data. The left image (a) illustrates two (visually distinctive) clusters where 20% of the data-samples are wrongly labeled. The color of the markers (red vs. blue) encodes the true label and the shape of the markers encodes the label for the supervised adaptation of a Learning Vector Quantization approach. The right image (b) shows the result of a systematic increase of the noise. This plot shows the baseline performance obtained by the unsupervised k-means algorithm, the GLVQ training error and the GLVQ testing error. Additionally the blue line indicates the amount of correct labels.*

Robustness of prototype-based models The prototypes of a GLVQ network are optimized by means of supervised online adaptation. That is, a random feature $\vec{\xi} \in \mathcal{D}$ is selected and the two best matching prototypes $\vec{w}_J$ and $\vec{w}_K$ are determined. Similar to the update scheme proposed by Kohonen the best matching prototype from the correct class is attracted and the one from an incorrect class is repelled.

The concept of prototype-based learning relies on the feature densities and the rate how often a particular type of feature vector is selected by random sampling. For this reason it is possible that the classifier can be adapted correctly also in the presence of noise, i.e. some of the data points are wrongly labeled. In this case, prototype-based methods gradually degrade dependent on the amount of noise and overlap between the clusters. Typically this behavior addresses the removal of prototypes from the network and is referred as graceful degradation (Howard 2004). Similarly the network performance is gradually impaired with increasing noise as long as the noise is randomly distributed. This can be exemplified by a toy-example illustrated in Fig. 3.2(a). In this figure a simple 2D dataset with two clusters is used. The true label $c^-[\vec{\xi}]$ of the data points to generate the clusters is encoded by the color of the markers (red vs. blue).

3.3. APPLICATION OF GLVQ FOR IMAGE SEGMENTATION

To adapt a GLVQ network a noisy label $c[\vec{\xi}]$ is used, i.e. some of the data points are wrongly labeled $c[\vec{\xi}] \neq c^-[\vec{\xi}]$. This supervised label is encoded by the shape of the markers (crosses vs. circles). In this example 20% of the data points of each class are assigned to the wrong class. An unsupervised model like k-means (Lloyd 1982; Bishop 2007) ignores the label of the data points and is capable to obtain the cluster structure with a classification error of 4% with respect to the true label. For this illustration the unsupervised model is used to provide a baseline performance and is not intended as benchmark for both types of learning paradigms. For more complex structured data the exploitation of additional information is beneficial and even necessary. The supervised model is capable to yield the same performance despite of the fact that the training error is 20%. In this example the training error corresponds exactly to the amount of wrongly labeled data. In Fig. 3.2(b) the results of a systematic evaluation on this artificial data are shown. Up to a significant amount of noise (approx. 35%) we can observe that the testing error is not affected by the noise and similar to the results of the unsupervised k-means algorithm. However this behavior of the algorithm can be regarded as function of the model complexity as well. If only two prototypes are used the complex structure of the data caused by the random labels cannot be represented by two prototypes. In this case the algorithm has to generalize to the prominent structures in the data, which are the two clusters. For this reason this behavior will we further investigated with multiple prototypes on the image data in Sec. 3.4.

Feature weighting with adaptive metrics In the simplest case of only one prototype for each class, standard GLVQ with the Euclidean metrics separates two classes by a linear hyperplane (the border of the Voronoi cells, Fig. 3.3(a)). This behavior does not change with the introduction of global transformations ($\mathcal{Q}_M^G, \mathcal{Q}_V^G$). The relevance factors of $\mathcal{Q}_V^G$ and $\mathcal{Q}_V^L$ yield an ellipsoidal-shaped, axis-parallel scaling of data points equidistant to a prototype. In the case of the matrix transformations (of $\mathcal{Q}_M^G$ and $\mathcal{Q}_M^L$) the distance computation is additionally shaped to a rotated ellipsoidal by taking correlations of the feature dimensions into account. Besides the weighting of the feature dimensions according to their relevance for the classification the most important aspect is the extension towards local relevance transformations. This introduces more flexible (non-linear) decision boundaries between each pair of prototypes, by using different metrics for them. This effect is independent of the usage of multiple prototypes, which yields more complex tessellations of the feature space (Fig. 3.3(b)). The adaptive metrics are of special interest for image segmentation due to the feature weighting capability that is important if similar features in foreground and background occur.

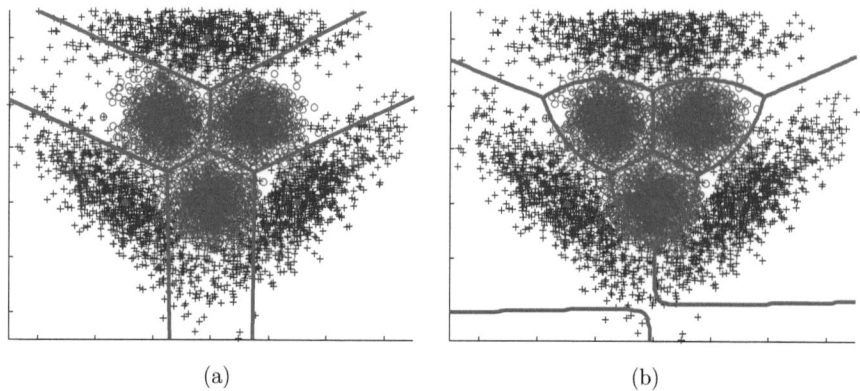

(a)　　　　　　　　　　　　　(b)

Figure 3.3: *In these plots randomly generated 2D data is used for the visualization of the Voronoi cells obtained by GLVQ. For the left image the standard Euclidean metrics was used while the right image shows the result of the localized metrics in $\mathcal{Q}_M^L$. From this figure it is visible that the localized metrics introduces non-linear decision-boundaries for only one prototype for each class. Hence more complex shaped decision boundaries can be obtained with a few number of prototypes compared to the Euclidean metrics.*

3.4 Simulations

In this section we analyze the previously discussed capabilities of the proposed model with respect to the intended application for figure-ground segmentation. That is, we will focus on the capability of hypothesis refinement, i.e. the capability of the classifier to cope with partially incorrect supervised labels (called noisy hypothesis). For this, the simulations comprise four parts. Firstly the baseline performance of the Generalized Learning Vector Quantization approach is evaluated. In this setting the impact of the different adaptive metrics is quantified and the most appropriate algorithm selected. Afterwards we will focus on the generalization capabilities of the selected method. In this experiment we gradually increase the noise in the segmentation hypotheses and compare the obtained foreground segmentations to the ground truth segmentations. This allows a quantification of the correctness of the segmentation as well as the degree of noise that can be compensated. We show that the method is capable to obtain improved foreground segmentations on the basis of the noisy segmentation cue. We conclude the simulations with two additional experiments to analyze in more detail the sensitivity of the model to the quality of the hypothesis. We show how the increasing noise level affects the feature weighting and we evaluate the robustness of the method with respect to the placement of the hypothesis, which is a particular source of noise.

3.4.1 Evaluation

HRI25 dataset of rendered objects This work takes place in the context of online human-robot interaction, which will be the focus of the Chapter 4. Hence for the most experiments the HRI25 dataset of rendered objects is used (Sec. C.2. This dataset is a compromise between a pure benchmark setting and a real world application. We employ a set of 25 realistic 3D objects according to our target application (bottles, boxes, cars etc.). For the rendered object sequences of 700 different poses of arbitrary rotation and the pixelwise ground truth segmentation $\mathcal{A}^*$ is available for each object-view. To present the objects in front of cluttered background the object-views are pasted in the center of a realistic non-rendered scene. In this video data a human presenter is in the background and his hand is near the object, see Fig. 3.4a. The video sequence is generated by tracking the view-centered hand in front of the camera system. More details on this platform will be given in Chapter 4.

Evaluation If the ground truth information is available, the segmentation quality can be quantified by a pixelwise comparison of $\mathcal{A}^*$ with the resulting foreground classification $\mathcal{A}$, i.e.

$$E_B(M_1 = \mathcal{A}, M_2 = \mathcal{A}^*) := \frac{\sum_{\mathbf{x} \in \Omega} |M_1(\mathbf{x}) - M_2(\mathbf{x})|}{\sum_{\mathbf{x} \in \Omega} 1}. \tag{3.10}$$

This pixelwise comparison does not take into account the variability of the foreground hypotheses (segmentation) in its size and proportion to the number of background pixels within the sequence of images. Therefore we measure the success of the segmentation by an increased overlap $E_O(\mathcal{A}, \mathcal{A}^*) > E_O(\mathcal{H}, \mathcal{A}^*)$ of $\mathcal{A}$ with the *ground truth* segmentation $\mathcal{A}^*$. The similarity function $E_O(M_1, M_2)$ normalizes the difference of two binary maps $M_1(\mathbf{x}), M_2(\mathbf{x}) \in \{0, 1\}$ by the sum of their foreground regions and discards the background pixels.

$$E_O(M_1, M_2) := 1 - \frac{\sum_{\mathbf{x} \in \Omega} |M_1(\mathbf{x}) - M_2(\mathbf{x})|}{\sum_{\mathbf{x} \in \Omega} M_1(\mathbf{x}) + \sum_{\mathbf{x} \in \Omega} M_2(\mathbf{x})} \tag{3.11}$$

This measure $E_O(M_1, M_2)$ yields a monotonically increasing function dependent on the overlap of M_1 and M_2. Note that, if the figure occupies only a small fraction of the image, then $E_O(\mathcal{A}, \mathcal{A}^*)$ and $E_B(\mathcal{A}, \mathcal{A}^*)$ can be significantly different, because the latter is mainly computed on the background.

3.4.2 Evaluation of adaptive metrics in GLVQ

In this first simulation we want to quantify the capabilities of the GLVQ algorithm on the image data to evaluate the importance of the different adaptive metrics implementations. Relevant questions address for example the effect of the increasing complexity of the metrics and the importance of the adaptation of prototypes compared to the metrics adaptation.

3.4.2.1 Experimental procedure

In this simulation, five implementations of GLVQ are applied to a foreground/background classification task on the HRI25 dataset (Fig. C.2). The implementations (listed in Tab. 3.1) differ in the usage of the adaptive metrics. To make a performance assessment we use the ground truth segmentation $\mathcal{A}^*$ that is available for each object view. In this setting the ground truth segmentation is used as initial segmentation hypothesis $\mathcal{H} = \mathcal{A}^*$ for supervised learning. That is, on a single image the networks are adapted according to the true segmentation. Afterwards each pixel of the resulting segmentation $\mathcal{A}$ is classified and compared to the ground truth segmentation $\mathcal{A}^*$. The obtained results can be considered as upper bound of the foreground classification performance and allows a conclusion which method is most appropriate for the classification task.

Parameter setup We achieve comparable conditions for all algorithms by the usage of the same parameter-configuration for all implementations. In this configuration the network consists of $N{=}20$ randomly initialized prototypes (5 for foreground, 15 for background). The decision on the number of prototypes for both classes depends on the image size, proportion of object size to the background and complexity of foreground and background. Most of the objects presented to the system consist of 3-5 different colors, which explain the choice of 5 prototypes for the foreground class. Note that this does not exclude single colored objects from the segmentation. Typically the background is more complex and cluttered than the foreground such that 10-15 prototypes are appropriate. This decision is supported by observations of Sun, Zhang, Tang, and Shum (2006). In Chapter 5 also the impact of an adaptive number of prototypes is investigated.

The GLVQ algorithms are applied to the image sequences of the HRI25 dataset in a framewise fashion. For each image the neural networks are adapted by 10000 training-steps (Sec. 3.2.1) to the changing image content. We have to note that the number of adaptation steps bases on the assumption that the image content from one to another frame does not change significantly. In this experiment the adapted network of the previous frame is used to initialize the network for the following image. This approach relies on the sequential character of the data and allows low number of adaptations on each frame. Also we observe that increasing the value of this parameter yield to a higher computation load but do not improve the performance.

The last important parameters are the learning rates to adapt the prototypes and the relevance factors. As stated in (Denecke et al. 2009) we observe that a fast adaptation of both prototypes

Method	$\mathcal{Q}$	$\mathcal{Q}_V^G$	$\mathcal{Q}_M^G$	$\mathcal{Q}_V^L$	$\mathcal{Q}_M^L$
$E_O(\mathcal{A}, \mathcal{A}^*)$	0.076	0.423	0.461	0.646	0.926

Table 3.2: *Evaluation on the rendered-object dataset with the multi-prototype setup (i.e. $\alpha = 0.05$). In this table the average similarity of foreground classification $\mathcal{A}$ to ground truth $\mathcal{A}^*$ for $\mathcal{Q}$ with different adaptive metrics is shown (5 repetitions on 25 objects and 700 views of the dataset). Here the perfect training data $\mathcal{H} = \mathcal{A}^*$ was used to adapt the classifier. For this $E_O(\mathcal{A}, \mathcal{A}^*)$ allows conclusions about the foreground classification error introduced by the methods itself. We can also observe from these results the increase in foreground classification performance that is caused by the increasing complexity of the metrics adaptation.*

and relevance factors strongly impairs the performance. By regular sampling in the parameter space spanned by the learning rates, we optimized the learning rates for $\mathcal{Q}_M^L$ towards $\alpha = 0.05$ for the prototype adaptation and $\beta = 0.005$ for the adaptation of the relevance factors. In this setup, to average the prototypes and matrices are effectively updated with values of magnitude around 10^{-4}. While this is moderate for the relevance factors, the prototypes with a range of $\xi_i \in [0..255]$ in the color components are slowly adapted, which is still reasonable on the large amount of data we use (300-700 images per object). In order to compare the effect of prototype adaptation and metrics adaptation, also regular sampling in the parameter space for the learning rate in GLVQ was used (Denecke et al. 2009). This yields $\alpha = 100$ for the input data we use in our experiments. Due to the dependence of the effective learning rates on the distance to the best matching prototypes (see $\frac{\partial \mu}{\partial d_K}$ in the update formulas described in Sec. 3.2.1), the average update values have a magnitude around 10^{-2}.

3.4.2.2 Experimental results

In this experiment the complexity of the adaptive metrics is the only modified condition. The proposed configuration of parameters yields to a slow adaptation of the prototypes and allows us to separate the effects of prototype and metrics adaptation. Hence we compare the impact of several adaptive metrics by exclusively varying their complexity and none of the remaining parameters (learning rate, number of prototypes). Previous results by Schneider, Biehl, and Hammer (2007) show that the performance of the GLVQ algorithm in classification benchmarks can strongly benefit from the usage of the adaptive metrics. From Tab. 3.2 it is visible that an increasing complexity of the adaptive metrics from relevance-vectors to matrices and from global to local ones clearly leads to an improved foreground classification performance and increased capability to compensate the reduced prototype adaptation. Measured by the overlap E_O that considers only foreground-pixels, the resulting foreground mask reaches an average similarity to the ground truth data up to 0.92 for $\mathcal{Q}_M^L$. In particular the results on the whole dataset give a

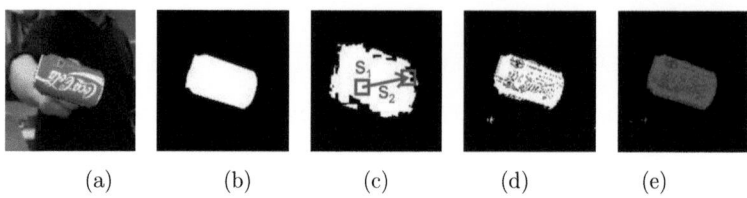

(a) (b) (c) (d) (e)

Figure 3.4: *Example image from the dataset of rendered objects and corresponding distortion of the ground truth data. From left to right the original image (a), ground truth $\mathcal{A}^*$ (b), distorted hypothesis $\mathcal{H}$ (c) with a patchsize $s_1 = 12$, shift $s_2 = 22$ and the resulting segmentation $\mathcal{A}$ (d) derived by a classifier trained on $\mathcal{H}$. Finally the visualization of the overlap of (b) and (d), which is quantified by the measure $E_O(\mathcal{A}, \mathcal{A}^*)$ during the experiments.*

more differentiated view on the capabilities of the different adaptive metrics. While $\mathcal{Q}_M^L$ yields a tolerable testing error (quantified by from the similarity $E_O(\mathcal{A}, \mathcal{A}^*)$), the less complex metrics adaptations are not appropriate for an application like our desired figure-ground segmentation.

Note that, although $E_O(\mathcal{A}, \mathcal{A}^*)$ can be very small for $\mathcal{Q}$, the overall pixelwise classification performance is much larger (defined by $E_B(\mathcal{A}, \mathcal{A}^*)$ in Sec. 3.4.1), e.g., 87% for $\mathcal{Q}$ and 98% for $\mathcal{Q}_M^L$. The reason is the large proportion of correct background classification versus comparable small number of misclassifications in the foreground region. For this reason the quality of the foreground classification is hard to assess from the measure E_B.

3.4.3 Hypothesis-based segmentation

On the basis of the preceding results we investigate the hypothesis-refinement capabilities of the $\mathcal{Q}_M^L$ algorithm. In this second simulation we analyze whether the foreground classification obtained by $\mathcal{Q}_M^L$ is capable to improve the segmentation compared to an initial noisy segmentation hypothesis. Like before the network is adapted according to a hypothesis $\mathcal{H}$ and the segmentation $\mathcal{A}$ is compared to the ground truth segmentation $\mathcal{A}^*$.

3.4.3.1 Experimental procedure

In this simulation the HRI25 dataset and the same parameterization as before is used. A $\mathcal{Q}_M^L$ network is applied to the whole dataset (25 objects and 700 views) but contrary to the previous setting the hypotheses $\mathcal{H}$ are generated by a scrambling method. That is, the ground truth segmentation $\mathcal{A}^*$ is used to generate artificial noisy hypotheses $\mathcal{H}$ (Fig. 3.4c). The distortion mimics the noise obtained from automatically generated segmentation cues like stereo depth or algorithms for optical flow estimation. This is achieved by randomly selecting and shifting 1000

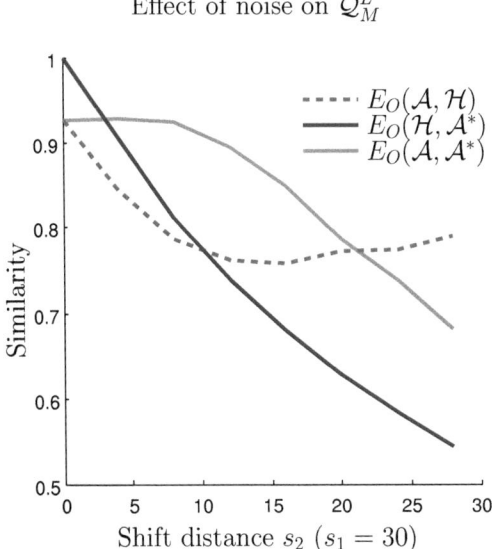

Figure 3.5: *This plot is generated by evaluating the foreground classification $\mathcal{A}$ of a $\mathcal{Q}_M^L$-network, which was trained on increasingly noisy hypotheses $\mathcal{H}$. These initial segmentations are generated from the ground truth $\mathcal{A}^*$ segmentation via a scrambling procedure. We measure the hypothesis refinement effect by means of E_O (Sec. 3.4.1).*

patches with size $s_1 \times s_1$ pixels from one position in the mask $\mathcal{A}^*$ to another by a randomly chosen distance between 1 and s_2. To address the capability of hypothesis refinement on the feature-maps $\mathcal{F}$, these hypotheses $\mathcal{H}$ are used as target labels for the randomly chosen pixels during the adaptation of the classifier. During the experiments we generate hypothesis maps with increasing noise by setting $s_1 = 30$ and increase the parameter s_2 from 0 to 30 pixels. The intensity of the scrambling and the similarity of the produced foreground classifications $\mathcal{A}$ to the ground truth data $\mathcal{A}^*$ and hypothesis $\mathcal{H}$ are quantified by $E_O(\mathcal{H}, \mathcal{A}^*)$, $E_O(\mathcal{A}, \mathcal{A}^*)$, $E_O(\mathcal{A}, \mathcal{H})$, as defined in Sec. 3.4.1.

3.4.3.2 Experimental results

In Fig. 3.5 the average similarities of the foreground classification $\mathcal{A}$ to ground truth $\mathcal{A}^*$ and the hypothesis $\mathcal{H}$ are shown (averaged over 5 repetitions of the experiment). We compare the similarity $E_O(\mathcal{A}, \mathcal{H})$ of the foreground classification to the data used for training $\mathcal{H}$. As the amount of noise is successively increased we can observe that for intermediate levels of noise, the foreground classification is more similar to the ground truth data than to the hypothesis (quantified by $E_O(\mathcal{A}, \mathcal{A}^*) > E_O(\mathcal{H}, \mathcal{A}^*)$). Furthermore the capability of $\mathcal{Q}_M^L$ to obtain a segmentation that is similar to the ground truth segmentation shows a graceful degradation with increasing noise (Sec. 3.3.2). Because of classification errors caused by the method itself (also observable in Tab. 3.2), some amount of distortion is required to observe the hypothesis-refinement effect. A further increase of noise results in a "learning" and reproduction of the hypothesis $E_O(\mathcal{A}, \mathcal{H})$, because the proportion of the object region is significantly reduced.

To explain the positive effect of hypothesis refinement, the number of prototypes and the introduction of the pixel position as additional features are important. The number of prototypes is constrained to be small and therefore the algorithm is forced to represent the most dominant structures in the image by means of this limited set. Important for interpreting the capabilities on hypothesis refinement is the fact that the noise induced by a wrong hypothesis is not randomly distributed over the image, but structured near the corresponding object. This noise, as well as similar colors in foreground and background, is responsible for overlapping clusters in feature-space. Transferring this feature into a higher dimensional space by adding the position alone does not solve this problem. Only the non-linear decision boundaries introduced by local transformations in connection with the even higher flexibility by using multiple prototypes for each class allow a better representation of this heterogeneously structured data.

3.4.4 Effect of feature weighting

Besides the robustness of the neural network to a noisy supervised segmentation hypothesis the second important aspect is the feature weighting capability due to the adaptive metrics. Therefore this simulation exemplifies the relevance determination in dependence on the image data and the amount of noise in the hypothesis $\mathcal{H}$.

3.4.4.1 Experimental procedure

In this simulation a simplified setup for the $\mathcal{Q}_M^L$, and $\mathcal{Q}_V^L$ algorithm, the localized adaptive metrics, is used. We constrain our investigation to a single image and a two class setup, each class modeled by a single prototype $\vec{w}_{fg}$ for foreground and $\vec{w}_{bg}$ for background. To achieve a better separation between the effects of prototype and metrics adaptation we set $\alpha = 0$ to adapt only the metrics. Further we select an appropriate sample from the dataset of rendered objects consisting of two nearly homogeneous regions (shown in Fig. 3.4a). This simplified setup offers the possibility to observe the properties of the prototype under changing noise-conditions and

3.4. SIMULATIONS

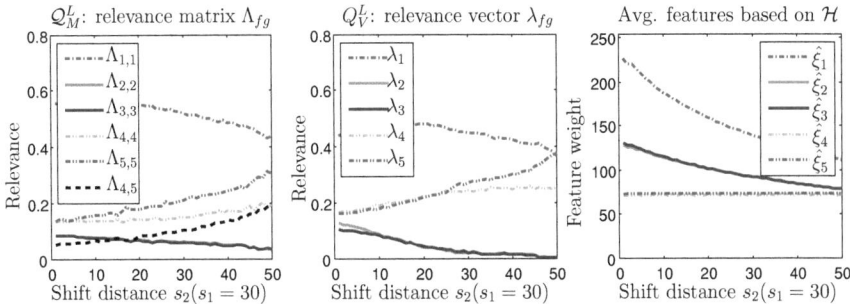

Figure 3.6: *Effect of noise on metrics adaptation of Q_M^L, Q_V^L on a single image with increasingly distorted hypothesis $\mathcal{H}$ (avg. over 25 repetitions). For Q_M^L the determined relevance values for the diagonal element of Λ_{fg} corresponding to the color and position as well as the interaction of the pixel position indicated by the off-diagonal element $\Lambda_{4,5}$ are shown. For Q_V^L the plot contains the components of the relevance vector $\vec{\lambda}_{fg}$. The prototypes are not adapted during this experiment ($\alpha = 0$) and therefore not shown.*

we do not need to account for interactions of multiple prototypes for each class. In this setting the prototypes are randomly initialized and not adapted.

For the generation of the plots in Fig. 3.6, the ground truth segmentation was disturbed by 50 levels of noise with fixed window size $s_1 = 30$ and gradually increasing shift distance s_2. To keep conditions on all 50 noise-levels constant, only on the first hypothesis (in this case $\mathcal{H} = \mathcal{A}^*$) the prototypes have been randomly initialized. This initial set is stored and used for the initialization of the network for the other 50 noise levels. For visualization, the averages of 25 repetitions with different initializations were computed. The average color/position features are computed according to

$$\hat{\xi}_i := \frac{1}{\sum_{\mathbf{x} \in \Omega} \mathcal{H}(\mathbf{x})} \sum_{\mathbf{x} \in \Omega} \mathcal{H}(\mathbf{x}) \cdot \xi_i(\mathbf{x}). \qquad (3.12)$$

3.4.4.2 Experimental results

Despite the limitations in the setup, the effect of increasing noise on the adaptation of the relevance factors can be visualized. In Fig. 3.6, the corresponding relevance factors for the foreground prototype $\Lambda_{fg}, \vec{\lambda}_{fg}$ as determined by Q_M^L (left plot) and Q_V^L (middle plot) are displayed in dependence on the increasing noise. With increased scrambling more and more background features are included in the hypothetical foreground region. That is, the properties of the foreground region are continuously changing as observable by the average color features $(\hat{\xi}_1, \hat{\xi}_2, \hat{\xi}_3)$ in the right plot of Fig. 3.6. As the noise especially affects the object contour, the objects center of mass $(\hat{\xi}_4, \hat{\xi}_5)$ does not change significantly.

Regarding the relevance factors, the advantage of metrics adaptation becomes visible with increasingly imprecise hypotheses. That is, the color features become less important than the position, indicated by the changes in their determined relevance. In this case, $\mathcal{Q}_M^L$ and $\mathcal{Q}_V^L$ are capable of adapting the relevance and increase the importance of the coordinates and their interaction. For $\mathcal{Q}_M^L$ this dependence can also be expressed by the corresponding off-diagonal element $\Lambda_{4,5}$. Hence with increasing noise the introduction of the position gets more important for the foreground classification which is the desired behavior.

3.4.5 Robustness with respect to hypothesis placement

With respect to the previous simulations an important property is the amount of noise of the hypothesis that can be compensated. The simulations on the HRI25 dataset give insights about the general performance and behavior of the proposed method. From the second simulation we can state that the method allows a robust figure-ground segmentation up to a significant amount of noise (measured by a similarity $E_O(\mathcal{H}, \mathcal{A}^*) \approx 0.8$ on the image data, Fig. 3.5). However on real world data several additional problems occur that cannot be modeled by a simple scrambling algorithm. Besides the noise of the hypothesis itself another important question is how the (dis)placement of the hypothesis affects the final result. The displacement of the segmentation hypothesis can be regarded as systematic error rather than the noise obtained by a scrambling algorithm that is equally and randomly distributed at the object region and boundary. We can expect that for two different hypotheses the result "converges" to the same segmentation if the algorithm is capable to determine the "correct" segmentation. This expectation is illustrated in Fig. 3.7.

3.4.5.1 Experimental Procedure

This simulation is applied on a real world dataset from a car detection scenario and is used to avoid the potential influence of an artificial dataset. For example the color contrast is in particular important for the feature-based modeling as the effectiveness of the approach depends on the discriminability of the colors in foreground and background. Dominant and highly saturated colors are easier to segment. In images of natural scenes usually the color contrast is less than for the rendered objects. The CAR dataset consists of a short sequence of 35 images, showing the rear side of a car and is in particular difficult due to the low color contrast between target object and background. A segmentation hypothesis was automatically

3.4. SIMULATIONS

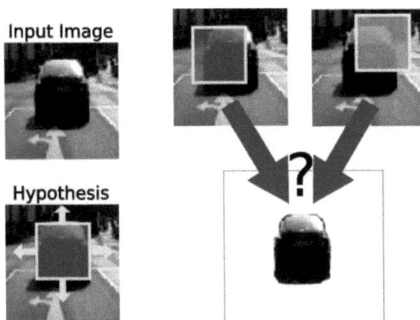

Figure 3.7: *This figure illustrates the experiment setup on the car detection data. For each image an initial segmentation hypothesis is available. This hypothesis is systematically varied in its position, i.e. shifted in horizontal and vertical direction to obtain several displaced hypotheses. The simulation aims at the question up to which degree of displacement the segmentation algorithm obtains a solution that is similar to the result obtained by the original hypothesis.*

generated by a car detection algorithm and is provided as rectangular region of interesst. For this data no ground truth segmentation is available (see Appendix C.5 for further details). The initial ROI was used to compute the segmentation $\mathcal{A}^0$. Afterwards several different hypotheses were generated by shifting the initial ROI into the four horizontal and vertical directions (see Fig. 3.7). The parameter "shift distance" again encodes the number of pixel for the shift. For each of the new ROIs the segmentation $\mathcal{A}^s$ was computed and compared to the initial segmentation with respect to the overlap $E_O(\mathcal{A}^0, \mathcal{A}^s)$. Furthermore the results are averaged over 10 repetitions of the experiment. Regarding the parameterization, two different setup were used, **setup (a)** with two prototypes and **setup (b)** with 15 prototypes (5 foreground and 10 background). In both condition the learning rate $\alpha = 0.05$ and $\beta = 0.005$ was used. The feature space consists of the RGB color channels together with the position features as usual.

3.4.5.2 Experimental Results

First of all we have to note that on this dataset only a qualitative analysis is possible due to the missing ground truth information. We investigate up to which degree of displacement the method is capable to obtain a segmentation that is as similar as possible to the segmentation obtained using the original hypothesis (Fig. 3.8). For the first **setup (a)** the algorithm shows the expected behavior. As long as the hypothesis is placed on a significant part of the object the result will converge to similar segmentations. Therefore also in this simulation the approach shows a robust behavior up to a significant degree of distortion. A small change in the hypothesis on average does not vary the result very much. The overall variance of the results is high in

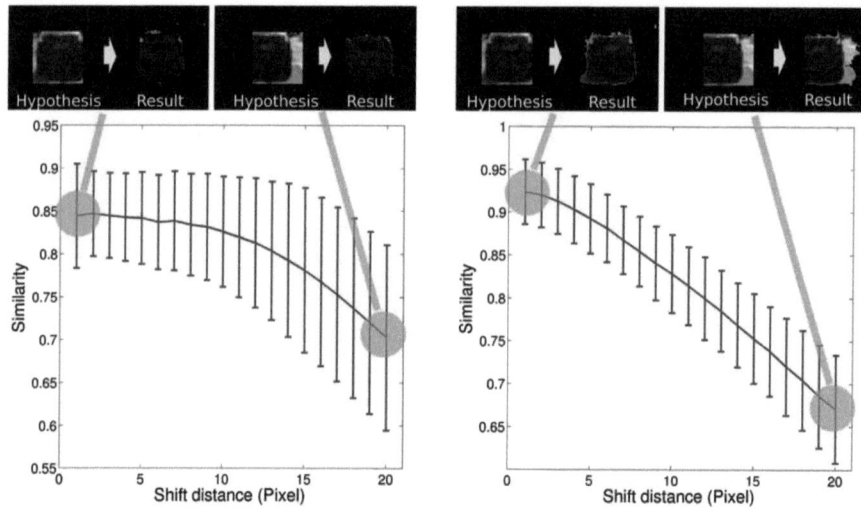

Figure 3.8: *Results for the two different setups using 2 prototypes (left) and 15 prototypes (right). The plots show the average similarity and the standard deviation of the overlap $E_O(\mathcal{A}^0, \mathcal{A}^s)$ of the segmentations for different shift distances. The top row shows examples for the hypothesis and obtained segmentation for 0 and 20 pixels shifts of the ROI.*

this setting due to the random initialization of the prototypes. From the results of **setup (b)** we can conclude that the robustness of the method depends on the model complexity. For one prototype for each region the solution has to converge to the two prominent colors of foreground and background. As the color saturation in this scene is very low the increase of the model complexity allows the representation of the wrongly labeled regions as well, which bases mainly on the position features rather than color values. The non-displaced segmentation hypothesis for each individual image and the corresponding foreground classification of the LGMLVQ algorithm for **setup (a)** are shown in Sec. D.1.

3.5 Summary

In this chapter a new method for hypothesis-based figure-ground segmentation was introduced. The supervised GLVQ algorithm and several adaptive metrics extensions were applied to image data in order to obtain a feature-based (Sec.2.2.1) segmentation into foreground and back-

3.5. SUMMARY

ground. The method aims for a prototype-based representation of both regions (Sec. 2.2.2.3) and focuses on two aspects, the robustness to noisy initial segmentation hypothesis and the feature weighting capability to discriminate between foreground and background. Both aspects could be handled by the Learning Vector Quantization approach due to the robust behavior of prototype-based models and the integration of feature weighting capabilities into those methods. In comparison to the state-of-the-art here a classification paradigm was used rather than the independent descriptive modeling of the regions. The method can be compared to the SVM-based approach proposed by (Xu et al. 2008). In their work the usage of a SVM is proposed to learn a classifier for foreground and background. Robustness to a partially wrong segmentation hypothesis can be achieved using an ensemble-based learning approach. The GLVQ model can be furthermore compared to the feature weighting algorithm for GMM-based region modeling proposed in (Wang 2007). In this work a scalar weight for groups of features is adapted similar to the Q_V^G model. At our knowledge in state-of-the-art methods for figure-ground segmentation both aspects are addressed by independent models like these.

To verify the capabilities of the model several simulations were accomplished and finally the LGMLVQ-algorithm was adopted for figure-ground segmentation. By the comparison of several adaptive metrics implementation we showed that the most complex metrics adaptation scheme is most appropriate for figure-ground segmentation. The introduction of prototype-specific matrices of relevance-factors leads to an improved foreground classification. In a second experiment we showed that the method is robust to noise, and is capable to improve the foreground segmentation up to a considerable amount of noise. Further simulation focused on the feature weighting mechanism and the robustness to structured noise in the hypothesis. In conclusion we showed that the method is appropriate for hypothesis-based figure-ground segmentation and the concept is robust against noisy hypothesis (distortion and displacement).

However, several open issues remain. So far the method was evaluated on artificial data and on the CAR dataset no objective evaluation was possible. Therefore until now we have not shown that the method is capable to derive a benefit on a real world application, which will be the focus of the following chapters.

Chapter 4

Integrated vision systems

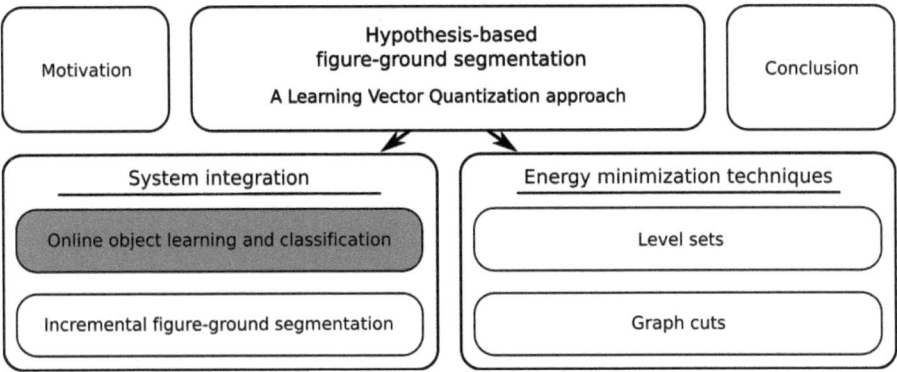

The problem of figure-ground segmentation has to be viewed in the appropriate context. The simulations in the previous chapter focused on certain aspects of the proposed method but do not allow a conclusion about the benefit of the image segmentation regarding its purpose for the recognition of the segmented objects. This thesis takes place in the context of human-robot interaction where figure-ground segmentation has the purpose to enable the construction of visual representation of objects. We begin with a short introduction and presentation of our research platform for human-robot interaction. Afterwards we will focus on visual representations for objects that were already roughly introduced in Chapter 2 and are the basis for two different integrated object learning and recognition systems. We will evaluate the benefit of the figure-ground segmentation method and quantify the performance of the segmentation with respect to object recognition tasks.

4.1 Introduction

In human-robot interaction, visual learning is an important component of artificial systems. It serves as basis to built-up a common knowledge about the visual world between the system and the human tutor. This enables the communication with human interaction partners and therefore a more complex behavior. To memorize the behaviorally relevant objects and the relations between them and their environment is furthermore a crucial step for the orientation in complex environments.

A particular important ability is the efficient and autonomous acquisition of new visual representations. If the goal is to achieve an unconstrained interaction, one has to take into account that such a system has to be able to build-up or extend their visual knowledge during interaction. This ability is referred to as online-learning and means the incremental adaptation of the visual representation to previously unseen objects in real-time and in contrast to static systems with a predefined, offline learning phase.

We outlined in Chapter 2 that figure-ground segmentation has a special role regarding visual online-learning. Its primary purpose is to focus the computational resources on relevant image regions and to reduce the data complexity for succeeding learning algorithms. The investigation of figure-ground segmentation in this context is of mutual benefit. On the one hand the usage of this scheme improves the learning efficiency. On the other hand this improvement can be measured to quantify the success of segmentation. Since figure-ground segmentation is an ill posed problem and its solution subjective, the usage in an integrated online system allows the investigation of such a method with respect to the task of the system.

In this chapter the previously introduced segmentation method is evaluated in the context of two integrated vision systems that were developed by our group to demonstrate the capabilities of our sensory feature representations for object learning and recognition. In both scenarios several objects are presented by hand in front of a cluttered background in a dynamically changing scene. The context of human-robot interaction imposes several challenges and constraints for the segmentation. First of all, for online-learning and recognition the segmentation method has to be capable to process video data in real-time since the segmentation is a preprocessing step for the succeeding learning algorithm. Additionally the method has to be complex enough to be robust under several environmental conditions, e.g.:

- Similar colors in foreground and background

- Changing lighting condition

- Specular highlights on the object surface

- Multiple moving objects

- Foreground objects from arbitrary and changing view-points

- Variations in illumination from one to another frame

- Low color saturation of the images

- Homogeneously as well as heterogeneously colored objects

- Partial occlusion of the objects

We argue that a hypothesis-based approach is most appropriate in this context. Following the general scenario shown in Fig. 1.1, we apply the Generalized Learning Vector Quantization with localized adaptive relevance matrices to segment the images as basis for online-learning and recognition of complex shaped objects. This hypothesis-based method is relevant for figure-ground segmentation due to its inherent robustness and feature weighting mechanism.

4.2 Vision systems for human-robot interaction

Several integrated systems for visual learning and recognition have been proposed so far (Goerick et al. 2005; Kim et al. 2006; Kirstein et al. 2005a; Wersing et al. 2007; Bekel et al. 2004; Arsenio 2004b). All in common is the general modular architecture that was already outlined in Sec. 2.1.2 and can be described on an abstract level by several components. These are a method to guide the attention of the system to a particular location in the scene that contains the relevant regions to apply succeeding methods for feature extraction and object recognition. This general architecture can be referred as feed-forward processing stream where the implementation of each stage differs for the particular instances.

The systems that will be described in this section build-up on the work presented in (Goerick et al. 2005). They focus on the attention part used to guide a robot platform and the handling of cluttered background for visual processing. In the first stage a camera system is employed that is actively controlled to explore the visual scene. This guidance relies on three levels of bottom-up attention: visual saliency, motion detection and depth estimation. The concept of peripersonal space is used to guide the attention to the user and to define what is relevant for learning, i.e. the object presented by hand. Without a further figure-ground segmentation process the resulting object ROI is fed into a feature processing stage. This stage consists of the biologically inspired feed-forward feature hierarchy proposed in (Wersing et al. 2003) together with coarse color information. Finally, a high-dimensional sparse feature representation of the input is obtained that can be fed into machine learning techniques to separate views of different objects. Object learning and recognition therefore take place on the highest level of multiple layers from simple to complex feature detectors. In (Goerick et al. 2005) a Single Layer Perceptron (SLP) was used for this purpose. The method was applied on a data set of 20 objects, each with 600 training views.

Later in (Kirstein et al. 2005a; Wersing et al. 2007) an online-learning version of this system was proposed, where a Learning Vector Quantization method was used instead of an SLP. This allows an incremental adaptation of the object classifier during user-interaction, which is referred to as online-learning ability. This Brainlike Active Sensing System (BASS 3.0) (Wersing et al. 2007) extends the previous work by several components like a figure-ground segmentation, a flexible memory architecture and speech-based user-interaction for label acquisition and system feedback. The build-up of an object representation is done online as well as the classification of the objects. In this system the segmentation obtained by a hypothesis-driven model (Steil et al. 2007) is combined with a hierarchically organized feature extraction similar as before (Wersing et al. 2007). This system demonstrates that during the interaction with the user the method is capable of learning the object representation on the basis of high-dimensional shape features. For this architecture it was shown that the performance of the object classifier is considerably higher with better segmentation from the background (Steil et al. 2007).

The second important system for our work is called BRAVO-1 (BRAVO: Brain-like Representation Architecture for Visual Objects). It is a further development of the BASS system towards an improved attention control (Bolder et al. 2007), alternative feature extraction and learning models. The BRAVO-1 system (Hasler et al. 2009) was designed to investigate a new feature representation compared to the BASS 3.0 setting, the "analytic feature" approach (see Sec. 4.3.2). In contrast to BASS 3.0 the system was trained offline and focuses on the identification of a large number of previously learned objects online and in real-time. During recognition, the objects are presented in hand in front of cluttered background as before.

The BASS 3.0 and BRAVO-1 systems are a possible basis for learning and recognition in human-robot interaction. Both systems are used as basis of our simulations where we will show that they significantly benefit from the used figure-ground segmentation scheme. In the following the components of these systems are described in more detail.

4.2. VISION SYSTEMS FOR HUMAN-ROBOT INTERACTION

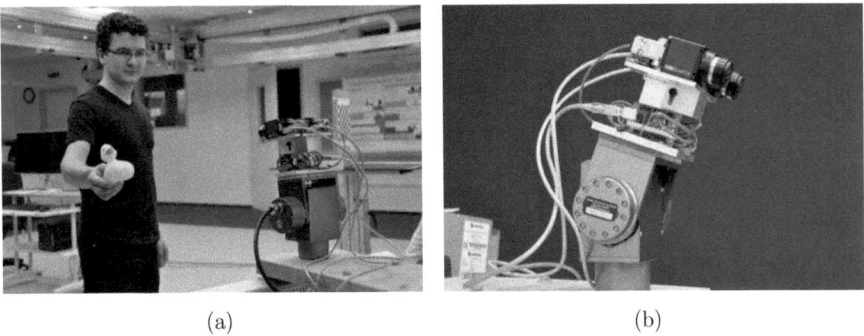

(a)   (b)

Figure 4.1: *HRI research platform. Left image: example of human-robot interaction. Right image: close-up view of pan-tilt camera head.*

4.2.1 HRI research platform

In Fig. 4.1 (a) the human-robot interaction of both demo systems is depicted. A human demonstrator presents objects by hand in front of an actively controlled camera system. This camera system Fig. 4.1 (b) provides the technical basis for BASS 3.0 and BRAVO-1 and was also used to acquire the datasets HRI50 and HRI126 as well as the background data for the HRI25 dataset. The system consists of a pan-tilt motor unit equipped with a pair of synchronized cameras (www.matrix-vision.com). The pan-tilt unit allows a ±90° horizontal and a ±60° vertical rotation angle. The cameras are capable to acquire high resolution images (800x600 - 1600x1200) with approximately 20 frames per second in the lowest resolution.

4.2.2 Data acquisition and preprocessing

After the acquisition of a synchronized pair of RGB color images a preprocessing is applied. In our demo system this is a gamma correction and a white balancing. Furthermore a good color contrast for the color-based modeling of foreground and background is achieved using the color constancy algorithm proposed by Pomierski and Gross (1996). These operations are referred as abstract transformation T_F of the feature map representation $\mathcal{F}$ (which was already mentioned in Sec. 3.3.1 but not specified in detail). Another important component is the acquisition of data-labels via speech recognition. During the presentation of the object the user can assign a speech label like 'toy duck' and this label is associated with the current data. The system can give feedback to the user by naming the object or indicate by 'unknown object' that the shown object is unknown or cannot be recognized.

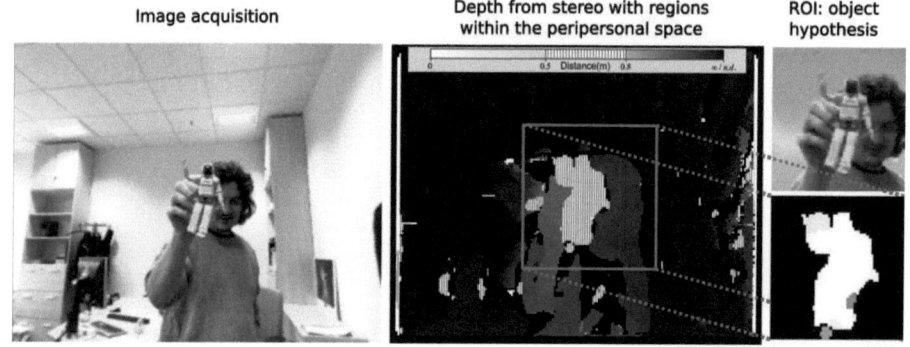

Figure 4.2: *Image aquistion using the concept of peripersonal space. The motion and depth information is used for attending and selecting the object during interaction. An initial segmentation hypothesis obtained from the depth cue defines which parts of the ROI correspond to the object of interesst. The highlighted region in the middle image consists of all scene elements within a specified depth interval.*

Attention system In BASS 3.0 the acquisition of the visual data takes place during an unconstrained interaction of the user with the system. For object localization and tracking, the pan-tilt head is controlled by a visual attention system. The peripersonal space concept (Goerick et al. 2005) defines the behaviorally relevant locations of the scene for learning and recognition. According to this concept, the depth estimation of the region in front of the system is analyzed with a blob-detection. This takes place within a specified depth interval (in this work 50cm-80cm), which is illustrated in Fig. 4.2. Via the control of the gaze direction the most salient blob is tracked by the system and centered in view. This facilitates invariance to the location of the object in the scene. From the blob-detection a square region of interest (ROI) is defined based on a distance estimate and normalized to a size of 144 × 144 pixels. Hence the same object, which is presented in different distances to the learning systems, will be processed with nearly the same size (size invariance).

An extended system on the basis of visually proto-objects (Bolder et al. 2007) was utilized for the BRAVO-1 system. Proto-objects can be thought of as coherent regions in the scene that are defined by color, motion or depth for instance. Similar to the concept before a proto-object can be tracked and referred to without identification and can provide an initial cue for object learning. This concept allows to track multiple proto-objects simultaneously while the previous concept is restricted to a single visual entity. However, in our setting only a single proto-object is used. Both methods provide a single ROI which contains the object as well as a large portion of the background.

4.2.3 Figure-ground segmentation

To neglect the background clutter the depth cue of the object ROI can be utilized as simple foreground segmentation. However due to the principle problem of 3D estimation from stereo data this depth blob is not sufficient for object learning. Typical problems are holes on homogenously colored regions and a weak approximation of the object boundary. The resulting segmentation errors are problematic in particular for shape-based learning methods. After the ROI is obtained a figure-ground segmentation is applied on this part of the scene. This stage consists of two steps, the formulation of an initial segmentation hypothesis and the application of a succeeding segmentation algorithm.

Hypothesis generation As shown in Fig. 4.2 the hypothesis bases on the depth cue that was already used to define the ROI itself. Instead of the direct usage a more precise segmentation hypothesis $\mathcal{H}$ is computed from the available depth and skin color information. In a separate processing stream for skin color detection (Fritsch et al. 2002) all skin-colored areas $\mathcal{S}, \mathcal{S}(\mathbf{x}) \in \{0,1\}$ are removed $(T_H(\mathcal{H}) := \mathcal{H} \leftarrow \mathcal{H} - (\mathcal{H} \cap \mathcal{S}))$ from $\mathcal{H}$ (Sec. 3.3.1). This is necessary because the hand is strongly connected to each object/hypothesis and can be regarded as systematic error.

Segmentation To segment the object on the basis of the available ROI and initial segmentation hypothesis, the method introduced in Chapter 3 is used. This segmentation concept can be directly applied to each frame separately. Nevertheless for computational efficiency the learned model from the former image is reused to initializing the set of prototypes on the following image. The reuse of prototypes on subsequent images accounts for the continuity of the image sequence and allows a reduced number of update steps on a single image. That is, after the initialization of the prototypes $\mathcal{P}$, this codebook is adapted for each succeeding image (Sec. 3.3.1) on training samples $(\vec{\xi}(\mathbf{x}), \mathcal{H}(\mathbf{x}))$ at randomly chosen image locations $\mathbf{x} \in \Omega$. The number of training steps was set to 10000 for each image. The number of prototypes and the learning rates are also kept as in Sec. 3.4.3, i.e. the learning rates of the prototypes was set to $\alpha = 0.05$. The learning rates for the metrics adaptation was set to $\beta = 0.005$ and the number of prototypes is 20 (5 foreground, 15 background). On the basis of the result presented in Chapter 3 we decided to apply the LGMLVQ method. Finally foreground segmentation derived in this stage forms the basis for object learning and recognition in the two following settings.

4.3 Feature extraction methods

On the basis of the segmented object views feature extraction and classification methods are applied. The BASS 3.0 and BRAVO-1 demo systems use different feature extraction techniques that were roughly introduced in Chapter 2.1.2. These are a feature extraction hierarchy for holistic object representation and the "analytic feature" approach (Hasler et al. 2009) to obtain a parts-based representation.

4.3.1 The feed-forward feature hierarchy

The feed-forward feature hierarchy is a type of artificial neural network that serve as model of the ventral visual pathway (Sec. 2.1.1) and can be traced back to the Neocognitron (Fukushima 1980). The intention of this model is to obtain a feature representation that allows robust visual pattern recognition. This is achieved by a multi-layer architecture with alternating feature detection and pooling layers. The topographically organized feature detection layers are composed of artificial neurons with increasing size and complexity of the receptive fields from one to another stage. Between two succeeding feature detection layers the spatial resolution is reduced by means of pooling stages. Neurons in this stage represent the activation of an ensemble of neurons of the preceding feature detection layer. These pooling layers introduce invariance to stimulus transformations like scaling, rotation and small local translations. The general model is not restricted to a particular number of stages. Finally an object view is represented by a high-dimensional feature vector at the highest stage of this hierarchy.

The model proposed by Wersing and Körner (2003) follows this general concept and consists of two stages with feature detection ($S1$ and $S2$) and pooling layers ($C1$ and $C2$). The input of the feature extraction hierarchy depicted in Fig. 4.3 consists of the gray scale representation $\mathcal{F}_I = \frac{R+G+B}{3}$ of the RGB image of the extracted ROI (Sec. 4.2.2). In the first feature detection layer S1 four different orientation sensitive Gabor filters $w_{s1}^i, i = (1, ..., 4)$ are applied:

$$a_{s1}^i(\mathbf{x}) = \begin{cases} |\mathcal{F}_I * w_{s1}^i(\mathbf{x})| & : \mathcal{A}(\mathbf{x}) > 0 \\ 0 & \text{otherwise} \end{cases}, \mathbf{x} \in \Omega \qquad (4.1)$$

The $*$-operator represents the application of the same feature detector to all images locations $\mathbf{x} \in \Omega$ similar to a convolution. The computation of the feature responses a_{s1}^i depends on an additional binary segmentation mask $\mathcal{A}$ that indicates the relevant foreground regions.

After the responses a_{s1}^i are computed, a Winner-Take-Most (WTM) mechanism between features at the same position is applied, which is followed by a threshold function. The succeeding $C1$ layer performs a pooling operation that reduces the original resolution to a quarter of the

4.3. FEATURE EXTRACTION METHODS

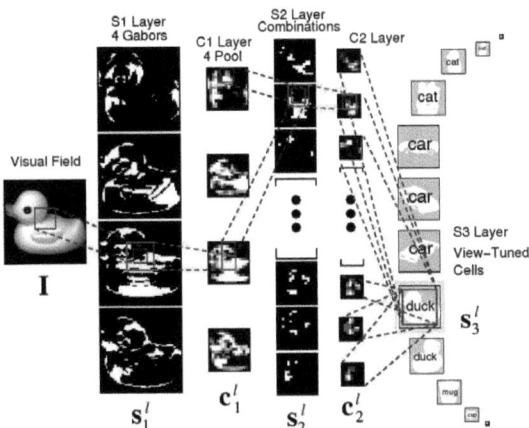

Figure 4.3: *Feature extraction hierarchy proposed by Wersing and Körner (2003). The gray-scale input is analyzed by layerwise feature detection and pooling stages. The S1-layer in this hierarchy applies Gabor-filters of different orientations, where the resulting response maps are fed as input to the next layer. After each feature detection layer the C-layer reduce the spatial resolution to achieve robustness to small stimulus variations like translation and scaling. In the S2-layer more complex combination features are detected and a high-dimensional sparse C2 feature vector representation is obtained in the last layer. Each object is represented by an ensemble of view-tuned units that correspond to prototypical C2-vectors of characteristic viewpoints.*

S1 layer. For this a normalized Gaussian pooling kernel w_{c1} (identical for all features i) and a sigmoidal nonlinearity (hyperbolic tangent function) are used:

$$a_{c1}^i(\mathbf{x}) = tanh(a_{s1}^i * w_{c1}(\mathbf{x})) \quad (4.2)$$

The neurons in the S2 layer are sensitive to local combinations of the responses in the C1 layer. In the proposed model 50 combination features w_{s2}^j, $j = 1, ..., 50$ are used that were obtained by a variant of Sparse Coding (Wersing and Körner 2003; Olshausen and Field 1997). The response a_{s2}^j of a S2 cell is computed according to

$$a_{s2}^j(\mathbf{x}) = \sum_i a_{c1}^i * w_{s2}^{i,j}(\mathbf{x}) \quad (4.3)$$

Therefore a neuron in the S2 layer integrates the input from all C1 layers. Similar to the S1 layer a WTM mechanism and threshold function are applied. Again a final pooling stage reduces the resolution to a half in each direction. The output consists of 50 $C2$ response maps that can be concatenated to a single feature vector. This feature vector is a high-dimensional representation of the input image and due to the WTM-mechanisms the feature dimensions are only sparsely activated. The actual size depends on the size of the ROI, which is 144×144 in our setup. That is, the $S1$-layer have the size of 144×144, $C1$ and $S2$-layer 36×36 and the S2 feature responses are down-sampled to 18×18 $C2$ features. Object-specific learning is only carried out at the highest level of the hierarchy (C2) by means of machine learning techniques (e.g. Single Layer Perceptron or Vector Quantization). The methods can also be applied without figure-ground segmentation $\mathcal{A}$ but due to its holistic concept the method takes great benefit if the background clutter can be removed from the object-representation.

Regarding the online-learning of visual objects we have to distinguish between the feature extraction on the input image by this hierarchy, i.e. the learning of the objects and the learning of the feature detectors of the hierarchy itself. While the feature detectors of the $S1$-layer are chosen on the basis of neurobiological knowledge (Sec. 2.1.1), the feature detectors of the $S2$-layer are the results of an offline optimization on a separate dataset before. Those features are learned in an unsupervised fashion to represent the statistics in the data and are of general applicability. The presented hierarchical representation was shown to yield good recognition performance on various databases and was successfully used in the online-learning system described in (Kirstein et al. 2005a). In contrast, the acquisition of the object representation relies on the C2 activations of a static feature hierarchy.

4.3.2 The analytic feature approach

The analytic feature approach (Hasler 2010) is an alternative feature extraction method that relies on a parts-based framework. Parts-based methods represent object classes or categories as collections of highly distinctive features. In this context a "part" refers to a specific structure of the object i.e. a configuration of line segments, color or texture or abstract representations of this. Illustrative parts of a car are tires, windows, headlights and side mirrors for instance. That is, parts are relevant elements that constitute the visual appearance of an object class and their presence is highly informative with respect to the classification task. Compared to the feature hierarchy before (Sec. 4.3.1) the analytic feature approach follows a different concept. This method aims for a set of feature that is highly distinctive to discriminate between the known object classes. Therefore a supervised learning paradigm is used on a dataset of labeled object views. This offline learning procedure has to be distinguished from the application of the feature detectors before. After a set of feature detectors is learned the activation of each feature on a particular input image can be computed by convolution i.e. compute the response at all image locations. The vector of maximum activations for all features can be fed into machine

4.3. FEATURE EXTRACTION METHODS

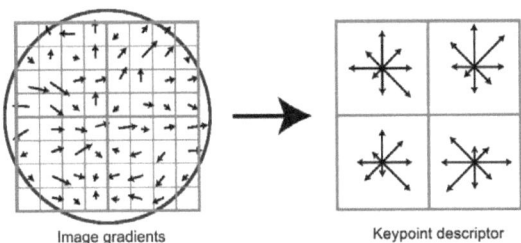

Image gradients　　　　Keypoint descriptor

Figure 4.4: *Illustration of a 2 × 2 SIFT descriptor, taken from (Lowe 2004). Around a image location in several sub-windows histograms are computed from the image gradient magnitudes and orientations. Before the magnitude of the gradient at each sample point is weighted by a Gaussian function to give less emphasis to gradients that are far from the center of the descriptor (left, indicated by the blue circle). In the right image the entries of the histograms are visualized by the direction and length of the arrows. The descriptor is formed from a vector containing the values of all the orientation histograms. To achieve invariance to illumination and orientation the descriptor is normalized to unit length and is rotated relative to the key point orientation.*

learning techniques for online-learning and classification. The BRAVO-1 system concentrates on online classification of known objects. However the analytic feature representation can also be applied in learning scenarios und the assumption that the obtained feature representation can serve as population code to represent new/similar objects as well. A comparison of these methods was accomplished in (Hasler et al. 2007b)

A parts-based approach does not rely on a particular feature representation. A straightforward and simple representation uses grayscale or RGB image patches. Such a representation provides a high specificity but is not robust with respect to certain appearance variations. The set of specific features has to be detected under several different viewing (affine or 3D viewpoint change, non-rigid deformations) and illumination conditions. Since image patches do not provide invariance to those conditions the Scale Invariant Feature Transform (SIFT) (Lowe 2004) was proposed. A SIFT descriptor is a feature representation at a distinct image position that takes a small neighborhood of pixels at this location into account (see Fig. 4.4). In contrast to image patches the method aims for a histogram-based representation of local regions of an image in such a way, that the descriptors are invariant to rotation and changing image intensity. The method proposed in (Hasler et al. 2009) utilizes such SIFT descriptors.

CHAPTER 4. INTEGRATED VISION SYSTEMS

Feature w_m	Image i 								
	Response a_{mi}	0.43	0.45	0.48	0.49	0.54	0.56	0.60	0.85	0.90
	Score s_{mi}	0	0	0	0	0	0	0	1	1

Threshold t_m

Figure 4.5: *Example score table for a single feature w_m (Hasler 2010). The images are sorted by the maximum activation a_{mi} of the feature w_m on it. The threshold t_m separates the views of a single class (e.g. the cup) from views of other classes that can be distinguished by the activation $a_{mi} > t_m$. To these views a score of $s_{mi} = 1$ is assigned.*

Feature selection Independent of the particular choice of the image descriptors Hasler, Wersing, and Körner (2007a) propose a feature selection method to obtain a parts-based representation. The algorithm assumes a set $\overline{\mathcal{W}}$ that contains the descriptors p_{in} of all image patches that are regularly sampled at all image locations in the training images. The index in refers to the location n of image i where the descriptor p_{in} comes from. e.g. patches of gray values. According to (Hasler et al. 2009) the derived SIFT descriptors that are computed for the training images are clustered for each image separately by means of the k-means method. The number of SIFT cluster was set to 200 for each of the 1000 training views per object and therefore 200000 × 126 candidate features are generated. To these candidate features the following selection method is applied to select 441 analytic features from this pool:

The algorithm is developed to obtain a subset $\mathcal{W}$ of features out of $\overline{\mathcal{W}}$ in such a way that objects of the training set are as best a possible separable in the feature space defined by $\mathcal{W}$. The resulting features will be referred to as being analytic, where this term should reflect the property of a feature to be specific for one or more classes, while generalizing over a certain view-space (several views of the object from different perspectives).

The response a_{mi} of a certain feature w_m on the image i is given by

$$a_{mi} = \max_n (G(w_m, p_{in})) \quad (4.4)$$

The specific choice of the similarity function $G(w_m, p_{in})$ depends on the kind of descriptor. In case of SIFT descriptors the dot product is used:

$$G(w_m, p_{in}) = w_m^T p_{in} = \sum_{j=1}^{J} w_m^j p_{in}^j \quad (4.5)$$

4.3. FEATURE EXTRACTION METHODS

The feature selection algorithm consists of two stages. In the first stage for each candidate feature its response for all training images is computed according to Eq. 4.4. Then a feature specific threshold t_m is determined, where $q(i)$ denotes the class label of image i:

$$t_m = \min\{t | q(i) = q(j), \forall i,j : a_{mi} \geq t, a_{mj} \geq t\}. \tag{4.6}$$

The purpose of the threshold is to determine which views of a certain class can be separated from views of other classes by this feature. Therefore images with an activation above t_m have to belong to the same class. Out of all thresholds that fulfill this requirement the minimal one is chosen. This determines how many views of the same class can be characterized by a response greater than t_m. Further a feature specific score $s_{mi} = 1$ encodes that a view i can be separated by feature m from all other view by means of the activation threshold t_m and otherwise $s_{mi} = 0$.

After having calculated the scores for each candidate feature $w_m \in \overline{\mathcal{W}}$, in the second stage the actual selection is performed according to the analytic quality of the feature, but also to the available object views. Difficult classes can be characterized by larger variations in appearance and probably are hard to separate by features with high generality. For each feature w_m a score s_{mi} is computed on each image. In difficult cases only a few object views exists with a score $s_{mi} > 0$. This is reflected in the quality function

$$E_A(\mathcal{W}) = \sum_i f(\sum_{w_m \in \mathcal{W}} s_{mi}), \tag{4.7}$$

with the Fermi function $f(z) = \frac{1}{1+exp(-3z)}$. This equation sums the scores s_{mi} over all images and all features in the set $\mathcal{W}$. A feature gets only a high score for images that were not separated yet (have no score for other features of the current set $\mathcal{W}$) and a much lower score for images in which features have already been detected. The set $\mathcal{W}$ is optimized according to a greedy iterative algorithm that starts with the empty set $\mathcal{W} = \emptyset$ and chooses in each step a feature w_m according to

$$w_m = \arg \max_{w_n \in \overline{\mathcal{W}}} (\sum_i f(\sum_{w_n \in \mathcal{W}} s_{ni} + s_{mi})). \tag{4.8}$$

Afterwards this feature is transferred from $\overline{\mathcal{W}}$ to $\mathcal{W}$ until a predefined size $|\mathcal{W}|$ is reached. To use this representation for object learning and recognition the activation a_{mi} is computed for all features in $\mathcal{W}$ on the given image. The selection of the maximum response for each feature transforms the image into an activation vector with dimensionality $|\mathcal{W}|$. On this representation standard machine learning techniques can be applied.

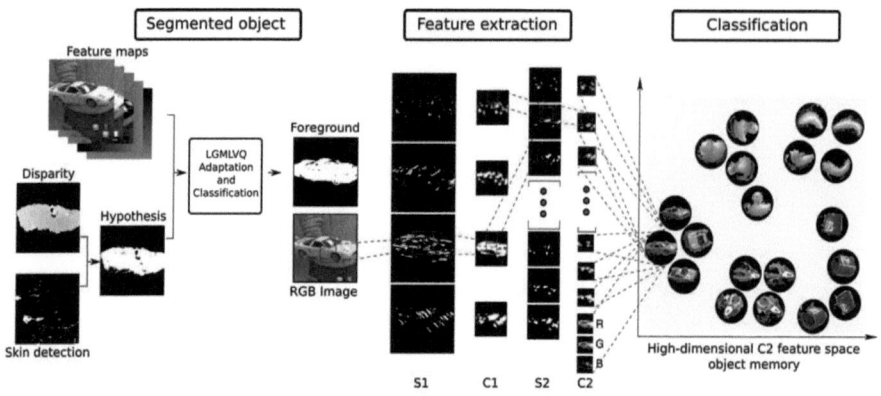

Figure 4.6: *Overview of the object learning part used in the BASS 3.0 system. Object learning and recognition are achieved by multiple stages that comprise image acquisition, figure-ground segmentation, feature extraction and classification. The initial segmentation hypothesis is obtained by combining the stereo disparity and the skin color detection of the available ROI (Sec. 4.2). The hypothesis together with the input image is used to obtain a figure-ground segmentation that is used to constrain the computation of the feature hierarchy to the object region. A Learning Vector Quantization approach is used to obtain a representation of prototypical object views in the high-dimensional C2 feature space (Sec.4.3.1).*

4.4 Simulations

4.4.1 BASS: View-based object learning and recognition

For the first simulation the Brainlike Active Sensing System (BASS 3.0) is used. The system follows the previously outlined learning architecture (Sec. 4.2) and was designed in order to investigate online-learning and recognition of objects during user-interaction (Goerick et al. 2005). An important part of this system is the feature extraction hierarchy providing the appropriate representation for object recognition. The original system architecture directly uses the depth cue as foreground segmentation for the feature extraction. In (Steil et al. 2007) was already shown that the usage of an advanced figure-ground segmentation scheme is beneficial for the online-learning performance.

On the basis of this previous work we investigate how this system can be improved by the proposed figure-ground segmentation. We focus on the object recognition performance to evaluate the importance of the figure-ground segmentation, to compare several metrics adaptation schemes and to compare to previous work. Additionally we also verify the hypothesis refinement capability (Sec. 3.4.3) on a large set of real world data.

The simulation takes place on a dataset that was acquired during an interaction with the system (Wersing et al. 2007). The HRI50 dataset Sec. C.3 consists of 50 natural, view centered objects with 300 training and 100 testing images without ground truth segmentation. To use a realistic setup, the training and testing data are acquired by different persons.

For the evaluation of the effectiveness of the figure-ground segmentation algorithm the architecture depicted in Fig. 4.6 is applied on this dataset. From the available depth and skin information the hypothesis $\mathcal{H}$ is computed without additional prior information on object position (as used in (Steil et al. 2007)). The image regions defined by the foreground classification are fed into the hierarchical feature processing stage (Wersing et al. 2007). Additionally to the 50 shape maps of the $C2$ vector 3 color maps that are generated by down-sampling the RGB channels of the input image (i.e. 144×144 to 18×18) are attached to the representation. Since we are interested in the object recognition performance rather than online-learning the final object classification stage is replaced by a Nearest Neighbor Classifier (NNC) in an offline setup. That is, in the training phase the $C2$-representation of each training image is stored and in the testing phase an image is classified by its most similar representative of this set.

In contrast to the evaluation on artificially generated image sequences the ground truth object segmentation is not available. For this reason the measure presented before (Sec. 3.4.1) cannot be used in this case. Instead the segmentation performance can be indirectly assessed by the overall system performance in object recognition or categorization.

4.4.1.1 Results

In this simulation several methods are applied, namely the depth-cue itself, the hypothesis $\mathcal{H}$, the ASDF (used from (Wersing et al. 2007)), and GLVQ with several adaptive metrics extensions. The resulting foreground segmentations are indirectly compared via the object classification performance of the NNC that is applied to the $C2$ representation of the segmented object views. In Fig. 4.7 we show several examples for $\mathcal{A}$ and the recognition performance achieved by the corresponding methods. In comparison to the baseline (using the hypothesis $\mathcal{H}$ only) and to the previously proposed ASDF model the recognition performance of real world objects can be significantly increased. From these results we conclude that the hypothesis-based concept using the foreground classifications of $\text{LGMLVQ}(\mathcal{Q}_M^L)$ causes a significant improvement in object segmentation. Regarding the different adaptive metrics schemes we verify the results obtained in Sec. 3.4.2. The increasing complexity of the metrics successively increases the foreground classification performance. To distinguish between metrics and prototype adaptation, $\mathcal{Q}$ with adaptive metrics was trained analogously to Sec. 3.4.2.1 with $\alpha = 0.05, \beta = 0.005$ primarily

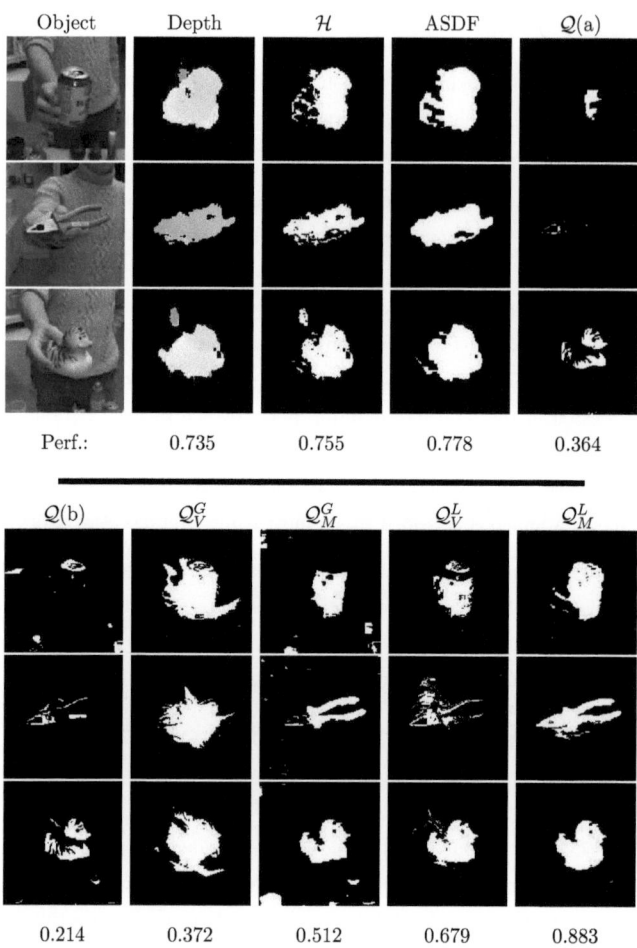

Figure 4.7: *From left to right: the input image, depth-map, hypothesis $\mathcal{H}$ and derived segmentation $\mathcal{A}$ using $\mathcal{Q}$ with Euclidian and adaptive metrics. $\mathcal{Q}(a)$ uses a higher learning rate of $\alpha = 100$. Bottom row, the average object recognition performance of a separate NNC on the high-dimensional C2 shape features (3 repetitions on 300 images for training, 100 for testing). Since the quality of the C2 representation depends on the object segmentation, we can observe a gradual increase in performance with increasing complexity of the metrics adaptation. More segmentation results on this data set are given for the $\mathcal{Q}_M^L$-algorithm in Sec. D.2.*

4.4. SIMULATIONS

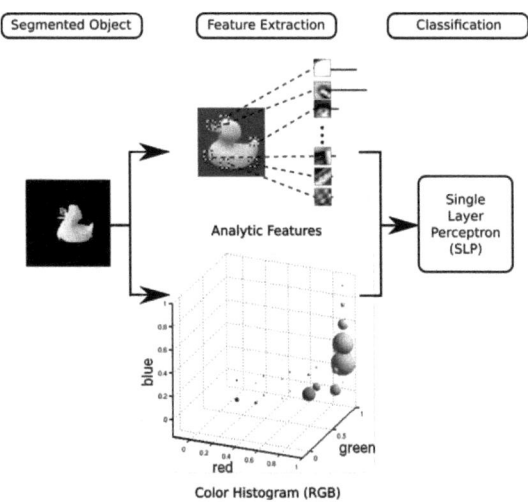

Figure 4.8: *Feature processing of the BRAVO-1 system (Hasler 2010). Similar to Fig. 4.6 multiple stages of processing are performed to achieve object learning and recognition. In this architecture the segmented object image is subject to a color histogram and analytic feature computation. Both types of features are combined to a single feature vector and serve as input for a Single Layer Perceptron.*

adapting the metrics. Also $\mathcal{Q}$ with Euclidean metrics was trained with two different settings. In $\mathcal{Q}$(a) a fast ($\alpha = 100$) and $\mathcal{Q}$(b) a slow learning rate ($\alpha = 0.05$) was used. In this setting we can observe that the default algorithm ($\mathcal{Q}$) is not able to cope with the noisy supervised data if the Euclidean metrics is used. Instead $\mathcal{Q}_M^L$ is capable of representing figure and ground on the basis of the most relevant features, which enables a correct foreground classification of the main object parts. We mentioned above that we utilize the components of the BASS 3.0 demo system to investigate the impact of different figure-ground segmentation methods. While the focus was not the online application of the system the results here can be transferred to this domain. Critical for this application is the runtime of the figure-ground segmentation module. The current implementation of this method achieves 7 fps in case of 144×144 and 10000 training steps on each image which is sufficient for online processing. This measurement was obtained on a 2.66 GHz Intel Xeon processor machine.

4.4.2 BRAVO-1: Parts-based object recognition

Similar to BASS 3.0 the BRAVO-1 system (Hasler et al. 2009) follows the architecture depicted in Fig. 4.6. In contrast to the BASS 3.0 this system focuses on the real-time identification of a large number of objects. The architecture differs in the feature extraction stage where the parts-based method (Sec. 4.3.2) is applied (Fig. 4.8). This method is more appropriate for this task due to its larger robustness against appearance variations of the objects (Hasler 2010). In this simulation we use the BRAVO-1 system to evaluate the importance and effect of the figure-ground segmentation stage on a different feature representation and dataset. Similar to Sec. 4.4.1 the performance of the object recognition stage again is utilized as indirect measurement of the segmentation quality. This quality assessment is used to quantify the hypothesis refinement and to evaluate the proposed segmentation method. This simulation took place in cooperation with Stephan Hasler. For large scale object recognition the HRI126 dataset was used, which subsumes the HRI50 dataset and 76 additional objects (Sec. C.4). Similar to the HRI50 dataset the image data contains a human presenter in front of cluttered background showing the object by hand. For each object 1200 images are available and an initial segmentation hypothesis is provided by a depth cue from stereo disparity. The evaluation on this dataset comprises two steps as before, the training of classifiers on the first 1000 views per object and the classification of the remaining 200 views.

The images of the training and testing corpus are segmented using the LGMLVQ-method ($\mathcal{Q}_M^L$) applied to the image data and initial segmentation hypothesis. The training of the classifier takes place on a bag-of-feature representation of the segmented object views. This feature representation consists of two feature types, a color histogram and an activation profile of a analytic feature representation. Color histograms are a simple and popular feature representation (Swain and Ballard 1991). Besides computational efficiency, such a representation is invariant to rotation and scale of the object views. To derive a meaningful distribution a reduced color space of only 6 bins for each color component was used. The histogram in RGB color-space with $6 \times 6 \times 6 = 216$ bins is normalized by the division with the highest entry. To achieve invariance to changing illumination conditions that can occur by moving the object in front of the system, the color constancy method proposed by (Pomierski and Gross 1996) was applied to the images. Additional to this simple color feature representation the representation of object structures relies on the analytic feature representation. After the figure-ground segmentation is applied, the computation of SIFT descriptors on a regular grid on the object region takes place. For each particular descriptor an activation map is computed and kept to encode the activity of each feature at all image locations. In this way the configuration of shape features is encoded with respect to the position in the image. The analytic feature approach only relies on the maximum activation of a feature and neglects the spatial configuration thus is more robust to appearance variation and deformation. In this work the activation of the RGB histogram bins are combined with the responses of a set of 441 analytic features to form a feature vector of dimensionality (216 + 441). For object classification a Single Layer Perceptron is trained on the feature vectors. In comparison to a Nearest Neighbor Classifier (Sec. 4.4.1), an SLP

4.4. SIMULATIONS

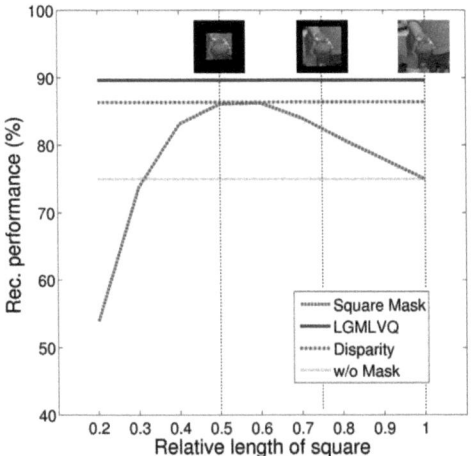

Figure 4.9: *Evaluation of different figure-ground segmentation schemes. To rate the quality the object recognition performance of an SLP on a analytic feature representation (Sec. 4.3.2) of segmented objects is used. The baseline performance is provided by the usage of the initial segmentation hypothesis and the foreground classification of a LGMLVQ-classifier. This is compared to the recognition performance obtained from different quadratic segmentation masks. For a relative window width of 1.0 the whole region is used for feature extraction (no masking) while for decreasing values only a smaller square inner image region contributes to the feature extraction. This plot quantifies the benefit of the proposed segmentation method compared to a prior segmentation cue like simple bounding box segmentation.*

consumes drastically less memory and has a slightly higher performance for the combined use of analytic and color features. This setting is also useful to investigate figure-ground segmentation since both kinds of features rely on object segmentation beforehand. Color histograms are global feature representations and are computed on the whole image. Also the activation of analytic features is computed on the whole image and in both cases the algorithm cannot distinguish between activation on foreground and background regions. Therefore the performance is strongly impaired in the presence of cluttered background.

4.4.2.1 Results

During this simulation an offline evaluation on the HRI126 is performed. After an adaptation of the SLP on the first 1000 view for each object the remaining 200 views are classified. In (Hasler 2010) the C2-feature representation was also investigated. There it was shown that the

C2 feature representation in combination with a Nearest Neighbor Classifier is not appropriate for this difficult data (recognition performance of approximately 30% for 1000 training views). Therefore in this work the impact of the segmentation is evaluated using the analytic feature representation. The results shown in Fig. 4.9 support the previous simulation (Sec. 4.4.1). Also in this case the usage of the proposed segmentation algorithm can yield an increase in performance compared to the usage of the initial depth cue (hypothesis refinement). The object recognition rate of the SLP is increased from 86% to 90%. Furthermore those results are used as baseline performance to compare to results obtained by a simple bounding box of predefined size, constant for each image. The size of the bounding box is varied in a range of 20% and 100% of the image width, positioned in the center of the image. The results depicted in Fig. 4.9 show that such an a priori assumption can be used if the size of the objects can be estimated beforehand and have a small variance. Actually this is not the case for such large amount of data and for online-learning and classification scenarios. The application of the proposed segmentation algorithm allows a larger flexibility as well as performance. Similar to the initial hypothesis used in Sec. 4.4.1 such simple segmentation schemes cannot replace the proposed method. Such heuristically settings can reach a similar performance (i.e. a minimum of 4% difference in the recognition performance) but lack the generality to be applicable in a wide range of input data.

The online application of this system was addressed in (Hasler 2010). In presence of a changing and cluttered background the system has to identify the objects in real-time according to the visual representation learned offline. With the feature representation using color histograms and 441 analytic features, the system is capable to accomplish this task with an acceptable rate of 6 frames per second. The limiting factor is the calculation of the analytic feature response for each possible location in the region of interest. As stated in (Hasler et al. 2009) this system is the first one that can identify more than 120 hand-held objects of arbitrary shape and texture in front of cluttered background, and thus marks a major contribution towards invariant 3D object recognition.

4.5 Discussion

In this chapter we focused on the application of the proposed segmentation method in integrated systems for visual learning. The general modular system architecture can be equipped with different segmentation, feature extraction and machine learning techniques for object learning and classification. We applied the proposed segmentation method on image data of two different demo-systems BASS 3.0 and BRAVO-1. Both systems were designed for online object learning and classification (Hasler 2010; Kirstein 2010) and differ in the used feature extraction

4.5. DISCUSSION

and object classification method. In both scenarios we were able to show the benefit of the figure-ground segmentation compared to simple segmentation concepts and alternative segmentation models. We verify, that the LGMLVQ method is capable to significantly increase the segmentation and indirectly improve the object recognition performance. In both simulations the object classification was used as indirect quality assessment of the figure-ground segmentation. Of course this measure strongly depends on the capabilities of the feature representation and the classifier that is applied to this data.

Regarding the simulations in the previous section the task-driven evaluation of the segmentation model verifies the results obtained on the artificial benchmark dataset (Sec. 3.4.2). In the BASS 3.0 setting the impact of the segmentation method was investigated with several different levels of complexity of the metrics adaptation. Similar to the previous results we could show that the most complex metrics adaptation scheme yields the largest benefit. In this evaluation the focus of the simulations was to show the advantage of figure-ground segmentation compared to other models. The simulations took place on real-world data and two integrated learning systems. The online application of both systems was not the focus of this section and is part of related work (Hasler 2010; Kirstein 2010). On our evaluation we could show the importance of the figure-ground segmentation scheme for both systems. The results here can be directly transferred to the online system. In (Steil et al. 2007) the improvement of online-learning was already shown, whereby in our work we could show an advantage compared to the ASDF method. The LGMLVQ-classifier for figure-ground segmentation can be applied in these online settings. The low model complexity and therefore efficient processing allows a real-time application on video data.

However, the performance of segmentation method relies on the number of prototypes. The model complexity directly affects the generalization of the classifier and the hypothesis refinement ability. A large number of prototypes may lead to over-fitting and will reproduce the inconsistent parts of the hypothesis as well. The model complexity is also a crucial factor for the runtime since the computational effort of the segmentation model depends on the number of model neurons. Despite of the model complexity from the results we can see that pixel wise classification is a very noisy process. So far the proposed method does not integrate topological or region constraints to obtain a spatially consistent result. Only the integration of the pixel position as feature integrates an implicit region concept to take the topology of the image into account. These issues are subject of the following chapters.

Chapter 5

The model selection problem

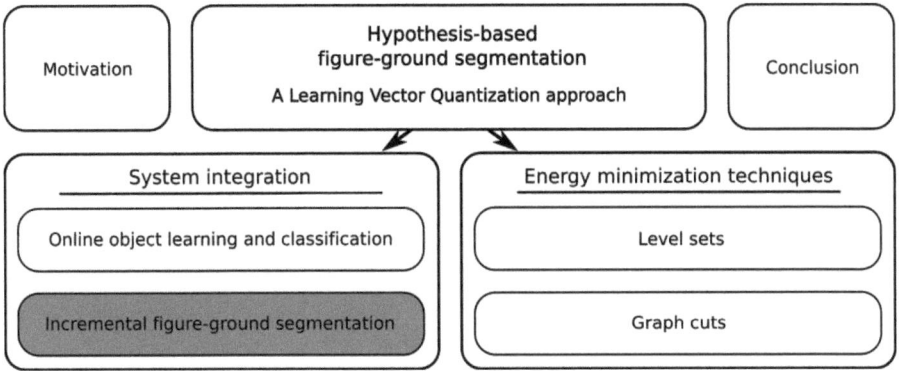

In general the performance of computational models depends on the appropriate choice of the model parameters. Commonly known as model selection problem, the choice of learning rates for instance, affects the capability to adapt the model to the continuously changing data. In the former chapter the two important parameters (learning rates and the number of model neurons) of the segmentation algorithm were predetermined on the basis of experience and regular sampling in the parameter space. However, a dynamic model complexity is relevant regarding possible over-fitting effects and computational demands. In this chapter we present an incremental approach to determine the number of model neurons in GLVQ (Denecke et al. 2009). After a short introduction we describe the method to allow incremental learning in GLVQ, i.e. define criteria to introduce and remove prototypes from the network. We evaluate the method on a real world segmentation task used before (Chapter 4.4.1) and compare to the previous results.

5.1 Introduction

The appropriate choice of the number of model neurons is a principle problem in vector quantization networks. As we use a prototype-based model in the context of image segmentation, ideally the dimensionality of the network should represent the different homogenous regions if a color-based feature space is used. This problem is ill-posed since data clusters are seldomly well separated and the "correct" number of clusters is not tangible for an analytical solution (similar to the number of meaningful visual entities Sec. 2.2.1). Several researchers propose heuristics in unsupervised or supervised settings to optimize the network dimensionality. Incremental learning is one possibility to adjust the amount of resources needed versus the clustering or classification performance. One criterion used for unsupervised algorithms is the distance of the features to their representatives, namely the quantization error. The criterion in Growing Neural Gas (Fritzke 1994) (and similar for the Growing Cell structures (Hamker 2001)) aims at a minimization of the quantization error and introduces new prototypes where the quantization error is large, guaranteeing that the introduction of new prototypes reduces this error. An appropriate stopping criterion limits the growing process. Supervised LVQ primarily aims at the minimization of the classification error which offers another source of information. For example Kirstein et al. (Kirstein et al. 2008) propose a heuristics to insert new prototypes at the decision boundary using the misclassified data points together with a distance criterion to determine the location for new prototypes.

In this chapter we investigate Generalized Learning Vector Quantization (GLVQ (Sato and Yamada 1995)) with adaptive metrics and propose a framework for incremental and online figure-ground segmentation that faces two problems. Firstly, the local adaptive metrics complicates distance-based criteria to place new prototypes. Alternatively we use the confidence of the classification instead. Secondly, the method has to cope with noisy supervised information, that is, the labels to adapt the networks are not fully confident. In particular we address the second problem by using a parallel evaluation method on the basis of a local utility function, which does not rely on global error optimization.

Incremental learning in prototype-based networks needs a mechanism to control the growing process in order to determine an appropriate number of prototypes. A widely used possibility is a global quality assessment that is computed after addition of a new prototype. After the network grew until a predefined maximum number of prototypes is reached (Jirayusakul and Auwatanamongkol 2007) the configuration with the best performance can be selected. Alternatively the growing process stops if the change in a quality measure does not significantly vary by adding further prototypes. An online scenario as well as noisy supervised information, which corrupt global quality assessments, prohibits such methods. In our approach the network size is controlled by a local utility function without a criterion of global classification performance

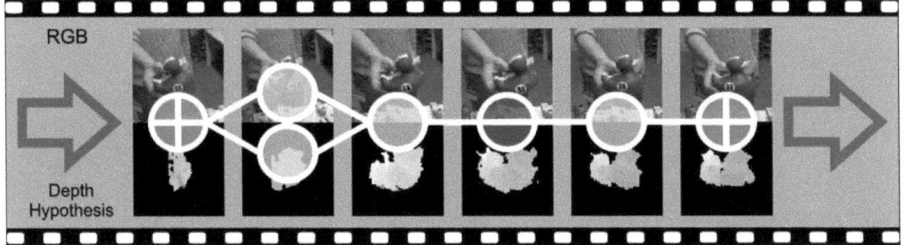

Figure 5.1: *The algorithm to adapt the size of the network comprises three steps. Firstly, a standard adaptation of a network using the LGMLVQ update rules (yellow circles). Secondly the green circles (plus) indicate an additional step to add a new prototype. This step yields two networks that are evaluated in parallel on the consecutive frame. Finally the red circle (minus) indicates an additional contraction step, where one of the prototypes (if appropriate) is removed.*

or measure for model complexity. In comparison to the work of Hamker (Hamker 2001) we avoid to use (non-normalized) distance-based error criteria for the insertion and removal of prototypes from the network which is attributed to the local metrics of the prototypes. We place new prototypes according to a confidence criterion on the decision boundary and rate this placement afterwards by the utility criterion.

5.2 Online figure-ground segmentation with adaptive network dimensionality

The proposed method comprises three components, a standard adaptation step, one method to add new prototypes and a local criterion to remove prototypes from the network (Fig. 5.1). To stabilize the incremental learning of the network in presence of the noisy supervised information, we use the temporal aspect of the data for a sequential processing (i.e. online) together with a parallel evaluation scheme. That is, to avoid the adaptation to the hypothesis on a particular frame, adding and removing prototypes are applied in a consecutive manner where on a single frame only one prototype is added or removed. The prototypes are added to a second network, which is an exact copy of the first one. After the adaptation and evaluation a decision is applied whether the original network or the modified network is kept for the following frame.

Network Expansion The first component of the algorithm has to specify when a new prototype hast to be added and at which location in the feature space. Due to the noisy supervised

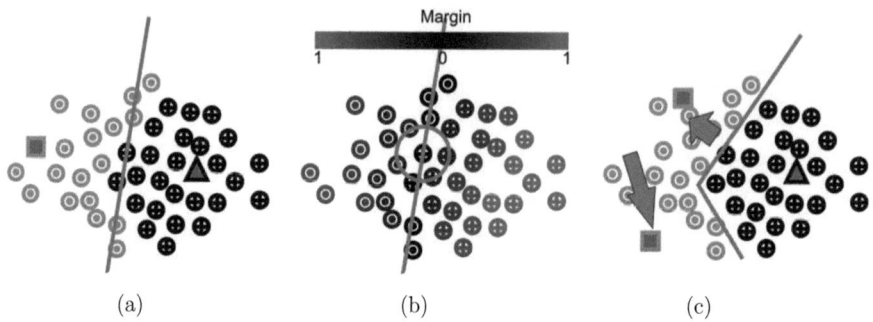

(a) (b) (c)

Figure 5.2: *Network expansion: To add a new prototype to the network (a), the classifier margin of all data samples ist computed (b). The data sample with the smallest margin, i.e. that is positioned closest to the decision boundary is used to initialize a new prototype. On the next video frame the postion of the prototypes in feature space is adapted to obtain a new decision boundary (c).*

labels a confident global quality assessment of the network is not available. Hence it is not possible to determine when it is necessary to introduce new prototypes and the proposed algorithm expands the network in specified time intervals. The decision where a new prototype has to be added can be based on criteria like the random insertion, a placement on false classified data or on the decision boundary. In prototype-based networks the decision boundary is characterized by the difference between the minimum distances of a data sample to the prototypes of the different classes. This difference is zero in case of equal distances which is the case for all locations in the feature space on the decision boundary. The objective of GLVQ is to minimize an error function which represents not only the classification error but also introduces an error term for unconfidently classified data points (Eq. 3.1) that bases on the difference (the margin) in the nominator of the function $\mu(\mathcal{P}, \vec{\xi}(\mathbf{x}))$ (Eq. 3.2). Utilizing the margin for learning was proposed in the context of active learning by Schleif, Hammer, and Villmann (2007) for instance. They propose that new data points for learning are acquired on the basis of the margin criterion. However this information was not used in the context of incremental learning before. Since the margin is implicitly optimized by the GLVQ error function, we decide to add new prototypes in these regions of low confidence, respectively directly on the decision boundary (Fig. 5.2). For each expansion step a new prototype is positioned at the training vector with the minimum normalized margin $\mu(\mathcal{P}, \vec{\xi}^i) = \frac{\|d_J^i - d_K^i\|}{d_J^i + d_K^i}, \vec{\xi}^i \in \mathcal{D}, i = 1,..,|\mathcal{D}|$. The label of the new prototype is initialized according to the supervised label, while the relevance matrix is taken from the best matching correct prototype according to this label. Since the network size adapted from one to another frame this operation provides an initialization of the network for the adaptation on the next frame.

5.2. ONLINE FIGURE-GROUND SEGMENTATION WITH ADAPTIVE NETWORK DIMENSIONALITY

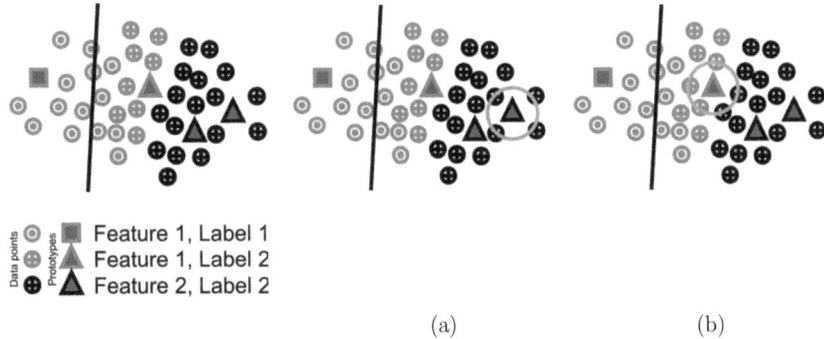

- Feature 1, Label 1
- Feature 1, Label 2
- Feature 2, Label 2

(a) (b)

Figure 5.3: *Network contraction: To remove a prototype from the network a local utility criterion is used. This criterion estimates how the classification performance is affected if the prototype is removed and all data samples are assigned to the next most similar prototype in feature space. Two cases are relevant for this removal: Illustration (a) shows the case where the removal of the prototype would not affect the classification since all data samples are assigned to a prototype of the same class. Illustration (b) shows the removal of a misplaced prototype. This is a prototype that represents the features of class 1, but due to a wrong label provided by the noisy hypothesis it is assigned to class 2. During the experiments we observe that the presence of such prototype can cause classification errors that are identified by the utility criterion U.*

Network contraction To rate the importance of each single prototype in the network a local utility criterion is used. For vector quantization Fritzke (1997) proposes to rate single neurons according to the quantization error of a prototype by the following utility function

$$U(\vec{w}_p) := E_{\text{glvq}}[\mathcal{D}, \mathcal{P} \setminus \vec{w}_p] - E_{\text{glvq}}[\mathcal{D}, \mathcal{P}] = \sum_{\vec{\xi} \in \mathcal{D}} \parallel \vec{\xi} - \vec{w}_s \parallel^2 - \parallel \vec{\xi} - \vec{w}_p \parallel^2 \quad (5.1)$$

where $\vec{w}_s$ is the winning prototype from the set $\mathcal{P} \setminus \{\vec{w}_p\}$. As the quantization error (which is also exploited by Hamker (2001) for a local utility function) is based on a global consistent metrics this method is not appropriate for localized adaptive metrics. This motivates a utility $u(\vec{w}_p)$ function on the basis of the classification error. For a single training example $\vec{\xi}$ this function is:

$$u(\vec{w}_p) = \begin{cases} 1 & c[\vec{w}_p] = c[\vec{\xi}], \ c[\vec{w}_s] \neq c[\vec{\xi}] \\ 0 & \text{else} \end{cases}$$

Finally, the utility of the prototype on the whole dataset is normalized by the number of activations

$$n(\vec{w}_p) = |\{\vec{\xi} | \vec{\xi} \in \mathcal{D}, d(\vec{w}_p, \vec{\xi}) = \min_{q \in \mathcal{P}} d(\vec{w}_q, \vec{\xi})\}| \quad (5.2)$$

of this prototype:

$$U(\vec{w}_p) = \frac{1}{n(\vec{w}_p)} \sum_{\vec{\xi} \in \mathcal{D}} u(\vec{w}_p). \tag{5.3}$$

If the value $U(\vec{w}_p)$ falls below a given threshold $t_u = 0.01$, the prototype is regarded as a removal candidate. After an expansion step, the new prototype is kept, if this one and all other current prototypes are useful (i.e. $U(\vec{w}_p > t_u \forall p \in \mathcal{P})$). This ensures to limit the network size to a number of useful prototypes. Independent of the utility function to evaluate the success of an expansion step, we use this function for separate contraction steps of the whole network to determine possible spare prototypes or misplaced prototypes. Spare prototypes can be replaced by another prototype without impairing the performance (Fig.5.3(a)). Misplaced prototypes can be characterized by an assignment to the wrongly labeled subset of data by the initial hypothesis $\mathcal{H}$ (Fig.5.3(b)). Usually in the application/segmentation step this causes that more image portions of the background are assigned to the foreground. These misplaced prototypes can be identified to cause a large classification error even on correctly labeled data and therefore reduce the overall segmentation quality. Together with the recorded activation $n(\vec{w}_p)$ we use the utility criterion to remove such prototypes. That is, additionally to the utility criterion a prototype is removed if $\frac{n(\vec{w}_p)}{|\mathcal{D}|} < t_n$, where $t_n = 0.005$.

Algorithm

1 Input and preprocessing:

- Feature maps and hypothesis from object ROI: $\mathcal{F}(\mathbf{x}) := \{F_i(\mathbf{x})|i = 1..M\}$, $\mathcal{H}(\mathbf{x}) \in \{0, 1\}$.
- Preprocessing of feature maps $\mathcal{F}$ and hypothesis $\mathcal{H}$, see Sec. 4.2.2.
- Init codebook and metric (on first frame only) $\mathcal{P} = \{\vec{w}_p \in \mathbb{R}^M | p = 1, .., N\}$ where $N = 2$, $\forall \vec{w}_p \in \mathcal{P} : \vec{w}_p = \frac{1}{|L|} \sum_{\vec{\xi} \in L} \vec{\xi}$, $L := \{\vec{\xi} | c[\vec{\xi}] = c[\vec{w}_p]\}$.

2 Adaptation (for T update steps)

- Find best matching prototypes $\vec{w}_J$ for the correct label, $\vec{w}_K$ for the incorrect label according to a randomly selected $\vec{\xi} \in \mathcal{D}$.

  e.g. $\vec{w}_J = \{\vec{w}_p | \vec{w}_p \in \mathcal{P}, d(\vec{w}_p, \vec{\xi}) = \min_{q, c[\vec{w}_q] = \mathcal{H}^i} d(\vec{w}_q, \vec{\xi})\}$

- Update prototypes $\vec{w}_{J,K}$ by means of $\vec{w}_{J,K} \leftarrow \vec{w}_{J,K} + \alpha \cdot \partial E / \partial \vec{w}_{J,K}$ with learning rate $\alpha = 0.05$ and similar the relevance factors $\Lambda_{J,K}$ with $\beta = 0.005$ (Sec. 3.4.2.1).

3 Evaluation: for all features $\vec{\xi} \in \mathcal{D}$

- Determine the binary foreground segmentation $\mathcal{A} = c[\vec{w}_p], d(\vec{\xi}, \vec{w}_p) < d(\vec{\xi}, \vec{w}_r)$, $\forall r \neq p, \{r, p\} \in \mathcal{P}$
- Compute margin for each feature $\mu(\mathcal{P}, \vec{\xi}) = \frac{d_J - d_K}{d_J + d_K}$.
- Compute utility $U(\vec{w}_p)$ and prototype activation $n(\vec{w}_p)$ (Sec. 5.2).

4 (Optional) Network Expansion

- $\vec{w}_{new} = \vec{\xi}^i$ where $i = \arg\min_{\vec{\xi}^i \in \mathcal{D}} \mu(\mathcal{P}, \vec{\xi})$, $c[\vec{w}_{new}] = \mathcal{H}^i$, $\Lambda_{new} = \Lambda_J$
- $\mathcal{P} = \{\mathcal{P}, w_{new}\}$, $N = N + 1$

5 (Optional) Network Contraction

- Select $\vec{w}_p$ with the smallest utility $p = \arg\min_{p \in \mathcal{P}} U(\vec{w}_p)$
- Remove $\vec{w}_p$ if $U(\vec{w}_p) < t_u$ or $n(\vec{w}_p) < t_n$, $\mathcal{P} = \mathcal{P} \setminus \{\vec{w}_p\}$, $N = N - 1$

5.3 Simulations

5.3.1 Experimental Setup

This simulation is an extension of the previous work in Chapter 4. Again we evaluate the capabilities of this approach on challenging real world image data and investigate the effort of the obtained object segmentations in the context of online object learning and recognition. We use the HRI50 (Sec. C.3) dataset for a comparison to previous results (Sec. 4.4.1). That is the data of the BASS 3.0 system provide the basis for this evaluation. From the available depth and skin information the hypothesis $\mathcal{H}$ is computed where all skin-colored areas are removed from the hypothesis $\mathcal{H}$. To compare the results with previous work, the segmented images are fed into a hierarchical feature processing stage (Wersing et al. 2007). For object learning and recognition a separate NNC is trained on the high-dimensional shape features of the first 300 images for each object (training set), Sec. 4.4.1. On the remaining 100 views for each object (testing set) the object recognition performance is evaluated for an implicit quality assessment of the figure-ground segmentation. The separation into training and test does not affect the segmentation method. The incremental segmentation is adapted on a subset of the pixel data for each single frame like before. The parameterization of the segmentation is kept as before (Sec. 4.4.1) while the parameters of the incremental extension are described in Sec. 5.2.

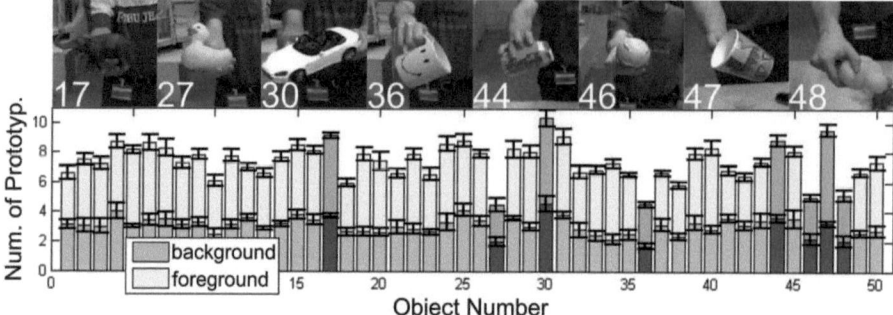

Figure 5.4: *This plot visualizes the network dimensionality for an application of the incremental segmentation method on the training-dataset (50 objects with 300 views). Each bar shows the average of 8 repetitions and 300 views each). On top, examples for eight objects with the highest and lowest number of prototypes are shown.*

5.3.2 Results

Network Dimensionality In the first part of this simulation the behavior of the algorithm is analyzed on an example of the training-dataset in Fig. 5.4. We apply the segmentation algorithm on the training set of the HRI50 dataset and draw the average number of prototypes in foreground and background for each object. To avoid an influence from the sequence of the presented objects, the order of the 50 objects was randomly rearranged for the eight repetitions of the experiment. On average over all objects 4.35 prototypes are used for foreground and 3.07 are used for background. Additionally the object specific standard deviation of the average number of prototypes for multiple repetitions is drawn. This shows that this number for a particular object is consistent over multiple repetitions of the experiment. The change in object identity yields an adaptation of the number of prototypes in particular for the foreground, which highlights significant differences for some of the objects dependent on their individual visual complexity.

Classification Performance Compared to a predefined number of prototypes in previous results (Tab. 5.1) three aspects are important: i) the general performance of the object classifier on the basis of the segmentation, ii) the used resources to obtain the results and iii) the variance of the results. Therefore we compare the incremental method to the results obtained by a predefined number of prototypes. In this case the static network size is chosen according to the average number obtained by the incremental method and the setup used in Chapter 4. On the basis of the same resources, a comparable performance is achieved (0.8742 using a adaptive network size compared to 0.8715 and 0.8828, compare to Sec. 4.4.1). Remarkably the variance of

N (#bg/#fg)	2(1/1)	7(3/4)	20(15/5)	adaptive	hypothesis
mean	0.7442	0.8715	0.8828	0.8742	0.755
std. dev.	0.0132	0.0110	0.0252	0.0036	n.a.

Table 5.1: *Results of the incremental segmentation scheme compared to previous results (average of 8 repetitions, except the last column). Dependent on the derived number of prototypes (on average 3 for background and 4 for foreground) the proposed method achieves a comparable performance to a predefined prototype setup, whereby the variance of the results is significantly reduced.*

the results is significantly decreased, which indicates a higher robustness to the noisy supervised labels. Together with a faster adaptation to the changing image data the incremental method also reduces the dependency on the initialization of the prototypes. Since the initialization for the fixed prototype setup was purely random, this can explain the beneficial effect. Compared to an offline parameter search the incremental segmentation might not be able to reach the potentially maximum performance (for 20 prototypes, 15 background - 5 foreground on this dataset), but offers an application to data with unknown "optimal" number of prototypes.

5.4 Summary

In this chapter we presented an incremental learning scheme for the GLVQ algorithm in the context of figure-ground segmentation. In presence of local adaptive metrics and noisy supervised information we use a parallel evaluation scheme combined with a local utility function to organize a Learning Vector Quantization with an adaptive number of prototypes. Due to the parallel evaluation scheme the expansion of the network no additional runtime was necessary since both instances were executed on separate processors. On our real world dataset we proved, that the incremental network is capable to achieve a comparable performance while maintaining a significantly smaller variance of the results, thus was more robust. In summary, the incremental approach to construct the network reduced the dependence on the initialization of the network. Furthermore the maintenance of an adaptive network size allowed an application without a regular sampling in the parameter space to optimize the performance of the network. Both properties are important for an application of the segmentation algorithm in an online-learning scenario with previously unknown data.

Chapter 6

Discriminative region modeling in level set methods and graph cuts

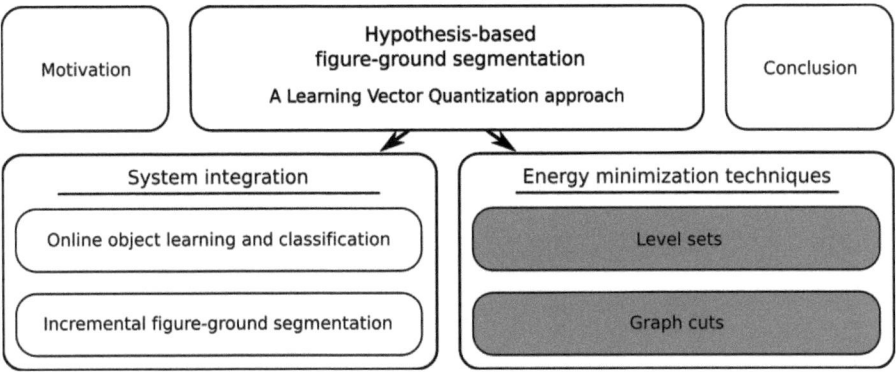

For figure-ground segmentation, the color statistics of foreground and background are the most obvious property to guide the image segmentation. However several other cues exist to distinguish the object region from the background. As pointed out in Chapter 2 an object is defined as something that has a definite shape, a property that is explored by shape-based techniques for object learning. So far this property was completely neglected in this work and also the topology of an image is only implicitly represented by the choice of the image features (Sec. 3.3).

The final chapter of this work relates the proposed segmentation method to established energy minimization techniques that are applied for hypothesis-based figure-ground segmentation. According to the categorization of segmentation methods in Chapter 2 the GLVQ algorithm is a feature-based technique to obtain a pixelwise classification of an image. Level set methods and graph-cuts provide the algorithmic basis to introduce region-based concepts and to consider further constraints for the figure-ground segmentation.

The remainder of the chapter is organized as follows. First we describe the state-of-the-art energy minimization techniques and show how the GLVQ classifier can be integrated in those techniques. The performance of the proposed methods is evaluated on a common benchmark dataset and we verify its competitive performance compared to other state-of-the-art models for hypothesis-based foreground segmentation.

6.1 Introduction

In Chapter 2 we gave an overview about methods that concentrate on different aspects of image segmentation and the special case of figure-ground segmentation. The usage of the GLVQ algorithm for hypothesis-based figure-ground segmentation can be regarded as feature-based image segmentation technique. That is, the properties of foreground and background are modeled in the feature space that consists in this work of color and position features. However due to variations in the image features the pixelwise classification of an image is prone to noise. Each pixel is classified independently of its neighboring pixels and their topological relationships are only implicitly represented by the usage of position features. This allows compact image segments but since the metrics adaptation can weight this features against the color, this is not guaranteed. In contrast to feature-based techniques the image-based segmentation schemes take further constraints into account, namely shape of the segmented object region or the similarity of neighboring pixels. Two prominent image-based techniques are graph cuts and level sets. The energy functions that are minimized in these frameworks typically take the region properties and contour constraints into account. To model the color statistics of the image segments, descriptive models like histograms and Gaussian Mixture Models (GMM) are widely used (Sec. 2.2.2.3). However these models do not provide feature weighting capabilities and the image regions are modeled independently of each other. This motivates to investigate the usage of the Generalized Learning Vector Quantization (GLVQ) classifier in these techniques. We build-up on previous work[1] (Denecke et al. 2010) and embed the error function of the GLVQ algorithm into a level set formulation. In this framework the classifier responses are used to determine the direction of the model-adaptation as well as the confidence of the classification to determine the strength of the adaptation. We expect that the discriminative feature weighting mechanism implemented by the metrics adaptation in GLVQ yields to a more precise region modeling, while the additional region constraint provided by the level set formulation leads to spatially coherent results. Compared to the separate application of GLVQ for image segmentation the level set implementation is optimized by means of several

---

[1]The work on the level set implementation was accomplished in cooperation with Irene Ayllon Clemente and previously published in (Denecke et al. 2010). The concept to integrate the GLVQ classifier and the implementation was contributed by the author and therefore is subject of this chapter.

iterations where the level set function and region models are adapted alternating. To verify the results and to show the advantage compared to established region modeling in those techniques also a graph cuts implementation is given. Both implementations are evaluated and compared to previously published results on a common benchmark dataset.

6.2 Methods

In the following, two different energy minimization techniques that are used for hypothesis-based image segmentation are presented. These are level set methods and graph cuts. Before we give a level set and graph cuts implementation that integrate the region classification of a LGMLVQ network we will give an overview of the methods, the underlying formal definitions and how to obtain a figure-ground segmentation.

6.2.1 Level-set segmentation methods

Level set methods (Osher and Fedkiw 2002; Osher and Sethian 1988) are one of the prominent energy minimization techniques used for image segmentation. These methods are a kind of numerical algorithms derived from active contours approaches, which are designed to track the evolution of contours and shapes. Active contours techniques (Kass et al. 1988) use local information measured around the contour by image gradient and global features as color and texture, which are analyzed inside and outside of the object regions to align the contour with the object boundary.

$$\phi(\mathbf{x}) = \begin{cases} \phi(\mathbf{x}) < 0 & \equiv \mathbf{x} \in \Omega_2 \\ \phi(\mathbf{x}) = 0 & \equiv \mathbf{x} \in \Omega^- \\ \phi(\mathbf{x}) > 0 & \equiv \mathbf{x} \in \Omega_1 \end{cases} \quad (6.1)$$

There are two approaches to represent active contours: explicitly and implicitly. Numerical methods using explicit representations try to track moving boundaries by putting a set of control points on the evolving contour and then modifying their positions to correspond to the changing boundary. In this case topological changes are possible by adding or deleting control points (Osher and Sethian 1988). In contrast to this, in level set methods the contour is implicitly represented on a regular grid corresponding to the image plane Ω. Mathematically the contour is defined by the level set function $\phi(\mathbf{x}) : \Omega \mapsto \mathbb{R}$ (Eq. 6.1). This function divides the image plane Ω into two disjoint regions, where Ω_1 represents the background region, Ω_2 the segmented object, and Ω^- the contour of the segmented object itself (compare to Fig. 6.1). The level set function represented by the conical surface in Fig. 6.1 intersects the X-Y plane

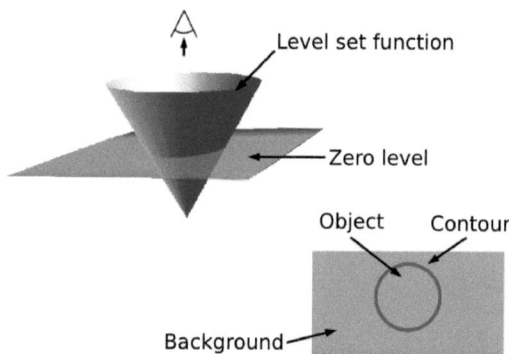

Figure 6.1: *Level set model (image taken from (Clemente 2008)). The level set function $\phi(\boldsymbol{x})$ as a function of the image position $\boldsymbol{x}$ returns a height defining a 2D surface. The cone-shaped surface intersects the X-Y plane at zero height, implicitly representing the contour of the object.*

and defines for each point $\mathbf{x} \in \Omega$ in the image plane a real value according to Eq. 6.1. Here the contour is represented by the set of all points that are at zero height, i.e. the zero-level of the function $\phi(\mathbf{x})$ (Osher and Fedkiw 2002).

Furthermore it is considered that the level set function $\phi(\mathbf{x})$ for a coordinate $\mathbf{x}$ in the image plane is negative for the region enclosed by the contour and is positive for the "outside". Evolving the level set function $\phi(\mathbf{x})$ changes the height of the surface at particular locations and therefore affects the contour defined by all locations at the zero level. In other words the evolution of the level set function is equivalent to the evolution of the contour itself.

Prominent formulations of energy functional for image segmentation were given by Mumford and Shah (Mumford and Shah 1989) and Zhu and Yuille (Zhu and Yuille 1996). Mumford and Shah use the mean gray value of a region as a simple region descriptor, which was later extended to vector valued data (e.g. color images, where $\vec{\xi}(\mathbf{x})$ represents the color values at position $\mathbf{x}$ in the image). This concept was adopted in (Chan and Vese 2001) formulating an energy function, where additional constraints on the contour length and region size are imposed:

$$E_{\text{ls}}(\phi(\mathbf{x})) = \sum_{i=1}^{2} \int_{\Omega} \chi_i(\phi(\mathbf{x})) \cdot (\vec{\xi}(\mathbf{x}) - \rho_i)^2 d\mathbf{x} + \nu \int_{\Omega} |\nabla H(\phi(\mathbf{x}))| d\mathbf{x} + \gamma \int_{\Omega} \chi_1 d\mathbf{x} \tag{6.2}$$

The unit step function $H(\cdot) : \Omega \mapsto \mathbb{R}$ is used to mask the regions and is part of the indicator functions $\chi_1(\phi(\mathbf{x})) = H(\phi(\mathbf{x}))$ that equals '1' when $\phi(\mathbf{x}) \geq 0$ and $\chi_2(\phi(\mathbf{x})) = 1 - H(\phi(\mathbf{x}))$ when $\phi(\mathbf{x}) < 0$.

6.2. METHODS

$$H(\phi(\mathbf{x})) = \begin{cases} 1 & \text{if } \phi(\mathbf{x}) \geq 0 \\ 0 & \text{if } \phi(\mathbf{x}) < 0 \end{cases}, \forall \mathbf{x} \in \Omega$$

Note, that for numerical stability regularized versions of the unit step function $H(\cdot)$ are used (Chan and Vese 2001). The region descriptors ρ_1 and ρ_2 are the average values of both regions, i.e.

$$\rho_1 = \frac{\int_\Omega \chi_1 \vec{\xi}(\mathbf{x}) d\mathbf{x}}{\int_\Omega \chi_1 d\mathbf{x}} \text{ and } \rho_2 = \frac{\int_\Omega \chi_2 \vec{\xi}(\mathbf{x}) d\mathbf{x}}{\int_\Omega \chi_2 d\mathbf{x}},$$

where the first term of the energy functional (Eq. 6.2) gets minimal for a grouping into homogeneous regions. Furthermore the length of the contour, represented by $\int_\Omega |\nabla H(\phi(\mathbf{x}))| d\mathbf{x} = \int_\Omega \delta_\tau(\phi(\mathbf{x})) |\nabla \phi(\mathbf{x})|$ in Eq. 6.2 serves as additional smoothness constraint and enforces that the contour Ω^- separating the regions Ω_i should be as smooth as possible. Finally the last term takes the area $\phi(\mathbf{x}) \geq 0$ into account (Chan and Vese 2001). The different terms of the functional $E_{ls}(\phi(\mathbf{x}))$ are weighted by means of the factors ν and γ.

Actually the level set function $\phi(\mathbf{x})$ that minimizes the given functional (e.g. Eq. 6.2) is unknown. For this reason the deformation of the contour is represented in a numerical form as partial differential equation (PDE). The level set evolution starts at a given position, the initial level set, and evolves in an artificial time. From the minimization of the energy functional (Eq. 6.2) with respect to the level set function $\phi(\mathbf{x})$ using gradient descent results in the following equation:

$$\frac{\partial \phi(\mathbf{x})}{\partial t} = \delta_\tau(\phi(\mathbf{x}))[\nu \cdot \kappa(\phi(\mathbf{x})) + \gamma + \lambda_1(\vec{\xi}(\mathbf{x}) - \rho_1)^2 + \lambda_2(\vec{\xi}(\mathbf{x}) - \rho_2)^2]. \tag{6.3}$$

This equation combines the evolution by mean curvature (Osher and Sethian 1988),

$$\kappa(\phi(\mathbf{x})) = \text{div}\left(\frac{\nabla \phi(\mathbf{x})}{|\nabla \phi(\mathbf{x})|}\right) \tag{6.4}$$

with the optimization of a single prototype ρ_i for each region. Further the regularized delta function $\delta_\tau(\phi(\mathbf{x}))$ with a smoothness parameter τ ensures that the level set is only adapted near the initial contour, the current zero-level (Chan and Vese 2001).

The algorithm starts with an initial contour (e.g. given by an initial hypothesis, compare to Sec. 3.3), which evolves towards the contour of the object by means of iteratively moving the contour according to the solution of the above partial differential Equation (PDE, Eq. 6.3). Hence to compute the PDE, an initial value problem has to be solved.

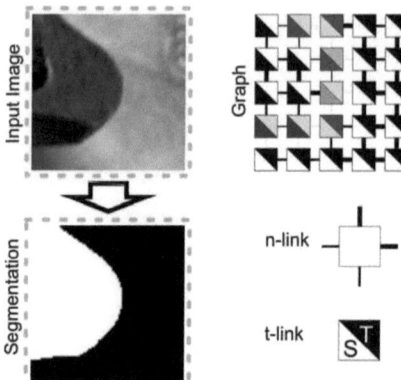

Figure 6.2: *Illustration of the graph representation for graph cuts. The graph consist of two terminal nodes $\{v_s, v_t\}$ (not explicitly shown here) and a grid of ordinary nodes representing the pixels. The nodes are connected by t-links and n-links, where the cost of each n-link is reflected by its thickness. The connection to the terminal nodes is indicated by the color of the nodes. Edges with low weights are preferred to be cut and the final assignment of the ordinary nodes to one of the terminal nodes determines the figure-ground segmentation.*

6.2.2 Graph cuts for image segmentation

The level set method described before addresses the segmentation problem in the context of implicit variational methods for contour optimization (Boykov and Funka-Lea 2006). A second prominent energy minimization technique that is applied for image segmentation are graph cuts. Graph cuts combine boundary regularization with region-based properties in the same fashion as the Mumford-Shah functional. Graph cut was first proposed by Greig et al. (Greig et al. 1989) in the context of combinatorial optimization for minimizing energy functions. It was applied by Boykov et al. (Boykov and Jolly 2001) for interactive image segmentation and successively extended in (Boykov and Funka-Lea 2006). The advantage of graph cuts is the efficient optimization of the energy function by standard minimum-cut/maximum flow algorithms (Boykov and Jolly 2001; Kolmogorov and Zabih 2002). The graph cuts framework also uses an implicit representation of continuous object contours but in this case as cuts on discrete graphs. The relationship between level sets and graph cuts is further studied in (Boykov et al. 2006).

The image is represented by graph $\mathcal{G} = \langle \mathcal{V}, \mathcal{E} \rangle$ that consist of vertices or nodes $v \in \mathcal{V} := \{\mathcal{O}, v_s, v_t\}$ and undirected edges $\mathcal{E} := \{\mathcal{N}, \{v, v_s\}, \{v, v_t\}\}$ between the nodes. In these definitions several types of edges and nodes are distinguished. The set of nodes consists of two special nodes, referred as to source v_s and sink v_t, that represent the labels foreground and background

(Fig. 6.2). The set of edges can be also differentiated into edges that connect ordinary nodes $\{v, u\} \in \mathcal{O}$. This neighborhood links (n-links) $e \in \mathcal{N}, \mathcal{N} := \{\{v, u\} \, | v \neq u, \, \forall v, u \in \mathcal{O}\}$ exist between all adjacent ordinary nodes. With respect to the image topology each pixel is represented by an ordinary node $v \in \mathcal{O}$ and neighboring pixels are connected by the typical 4-way or 8-way connectivity. Edges that connect each node v to the terminal nodes e.g. $\{\{v, v_s\}, \{v, v_t\}\} \, \forall v \in \mathcal{O}$ are reffered as terminal links (t-links). To each of the edges $e \in \mathcal{E}$ a weight w_e is assigned that corresponds to the cost to cut this edge. A cut of the graph is a subset of edges $\mathcal{C} \subset \mathcal{E}$ such that there is no path from one terminal to the other using the remaining edges, i.e. $\mathcal{G(C)} = \langle \mathcal{V}, \mathcal{E} \backslash \mathcal{C} \rangle$. To each of the possible cuts a cost is defined by the edges that are removed (Boykov and Jolly 2001):

$$|\mathcal{C}| = \sum_{e \in \mathcal{C}} w_e. \qquad (6.5)$$

Equivalent to the cut $\mathcal{C}$, a binary label for each node $v \in \mathcal{V}$ is assigned that is represented by a vector $\mathcal{A} = (\mathcal{A}_1, ..., \mathcal{A}_v, ..., \mathcal{A}_{|\mathcal{O}|})$. This vector $\mathcal{A}_v$ specifies the assignment of the ordinary nodes to the terminals foreground or background. In this way $\mathcal{A}$ defines the segmentation and the corresponding cost of a particular cut can be expressed (Kolmogorov and Zabih 2002) by the energy:

$$E_{\text{gc}}(\mathcal{A}) = \lambda \cdot \sum_{v \in \mathcal{V}} \text{Reg}(\mathcal{A}_v) + \sum_{v, u \in \mathcal{E}} \text{Bound}(\mathcal{A}_v, \mathcal{A}_u). \qquad (6.6)$$

This energy function consists of two terms. $\text{Reg}(\cdot)$ typically represents the cost to assign a node to a particular region (foreground or background) and $\text{Bound}(\cdot)$ denotes the cost for cutting the link between the adjacent nodes v and u, i.e. it assigns the labels $\mathcal{A}_v, \mathcal{A}_u$ to them. For example if two nodes v and u represent similar colors in the image, than a high cost is induced by disconnecting those nodes. The concrete formulation of those terms depends on the chosen method. For example the boundary cost can be chosen as:

$$\text{Bound}(\mathcal{A}_v, \mathcal{A}_u) = exp\left(\frac{-\beta(\vec{\xi}_v - \vec{\xi}_u)^2}{\text{distance}\{v, u\}}\right), \qquad (6.7)$$

where β can be set to $\beta = 1/2\sigma^2$ (Boykov and Jolly 2001) or $\beta = 1/(2\langle(\vec{\xi}_v - \vec{\xi}_u)^2\rangle)$. The $\langle \cdot \rangle$ operator denotes the expectation over an image (Rother et al. 2004). While the boundary term penalizes a cut through homogenous colored regions, the region term enforces the consistence of the region itself. A straightforward interpretation of the region term is the probability of a pixel to belong to the foreground or background model and to penalize an assignment by the negative log-likelihoods:

$$\begin{aligned}\text{Reg}(\mathcal{A}_v = \text{foreground}) &= -ln(P(\vec{\xi}_v|\text{foreground})) \\ \text{Reg}(\mathcal{A}_v = \text{background}) &= -ln(P(\vec{\xi}_v|\text{background}))\end{aligned} \qquad (6.8)$$

To model the intensity distribution for foreground and background, histograms (Boykov and Jolly 2001; Vicente et al. 2009) can be used. However, the usage of Gaussian Mixture Models has been recently established for this purpose, e.g. (Lempitsky et al. 2009; Rother et al. 2004; Blake and Torr 2004). Then $Reg(\cdot)$ is formulated as:

$$Reg(\cdot) = -log(\pi(\mathbf{x})) + \frac{1}{2}log(\det \sigma(\mathbf{x})) + \frac{1}{2}(\vec{\xi}(\mathbf{x}) - \vec{\mu}(\mathbf{x}))^T \Sigma(\mathbf{x})(\vec{\xi}(\mathbf{x}) - \vec{\mu}(\mathbf{x})), \quad (6.9)$$

where an unique GMM component (consisting of a weighting π, a center $\vec{\mu}$ and a full-covariance matrix Σ) of the region model is assigned to each pixel. To find a partition of the graph the individual costs are assigned to the nodes and edges. Then a standard graph cuts algorithm from combinatorial optimization is applied. For graphs with two terminals the global minimum is computed efficiently in polynomial time using the min-cut/max-flow algorithms (Boykov and Kolmogorov 2001; Ford and Fulkerson 1962; Goldberg and Tarjan 1986).

6.3 Integration of LGMLVQ

On the basis of the previous results (Sec. 3.4.2, Sec. 4.4.1) we decide to integrate the LGMLVQ-classifier into those methods. Compared to standard GLVQ the improved algorithm with metrics adaptation is capable to dynamically weight the feature dimension to optimize the classification performance. The structure of this model is very similar to Gaussian Mixture Models. In contrast to independent modeling of foreground of background the neural networks-based approach directly aims for the discrimination of both regions.

6.3.1 Level set formulation

To model the statistics of foreground and background several methods can be used for the regions descriptors ρ (Eq. 6.2). Instead of using descriptive models like histograms (Li and Xiao 2009; Weiler and Eggert 2007) we propose to integrate the concept of classification where the target is to derive two regions that can be well separated. The model of vector quantization itself is very similar to the region descriptors ρ used in (Chan and Vese 2001; Mumford and Shah 1989), where only one prototype (the average) is used to represent each region (Eq. 6.2). Therefore the usage of an LVQ network can be regarded as the generalization towards multiple region descriptors for each class. The advantage of using multi-prototype descriptors is that this method does not require two homogenous (piecewise constant (Mumford and Shah 1989)) regions in the image and it can also cope with heterogeneous appearance of object and background. To give a level set formulation, the error function E_{glvq} (Eq. 3.1) is extended by the contour term as:

$$E_{\text{lsI}}(\phi(\mathbf{x})) = \int_\Omega \frac{1}{1+e^{-\mu(\mathcal{P},\vec{\xi}(\mathbf{x}))}} d\mathbf{x} + \nu \cdot \int_\Omega |\nabla H(\phi)| d\mathbf{x} \quad (6.10)$$

The first term corresponds to the classification error where the sum over all pixels is replaced by the integral over the level set function $\phi(\mathbf{x})$. This error term gets minimal if both regions are well represented and discriminated. The second term, a standard contour term for level set methods, prefers short contours. To minimize the proposed level set functional, the gradient can be approximated as:

$$\frac{\partial \phi}{\partial t} = \delta(\phi)[\nu \cdot \kappa(\phi(\mathbf{x})) - C(\phi) \cdot \mu(\mathcal{P},\vec{\xi}(\mathbf{x})) + (1-C(\phi)) \cdot \mu(\mathcal{P},\vec{\xi}(\mathbf{x}))] \quad (6.11)$$

The method combines the evolution by mean curvature (Osher and Sethian 1988) (i.e. $\frac{\partial \phi}{\partial t} = |\nabla \phi| div(\frac{\nabla \phi}{|\nabla \phi|})$, Eq. 6.4) with a region term analogue to Eq. 6.2. Non-formally described, the level set function is modified by the confidence of the classification, represented by the margin (Sec. 3.2, Eq. 3.2). In regions where the classification is very confident, indicated by a large margin, a strong adaptation occurs in the direction estimated by the classifier (indicated by $C(\phi)$, where $C(\phi) = 1$ if the pixel is classified as foreground and 0 otherwise). The level set is only weakly adapted if the feature/pixel cannot be discriminated clearly. This formulation differs in two aspects from Eq. 6.2. Firstly, the models are not updated according to the level set function itself, but the classifier responses (using $C(\phi(\mathbf{x}))$ instead of $H(\phi(\mathbf{x}))$) to determine the direction of adaptation. Secondly, the update differs from this formulation, where not the difference to the prototypes is used, but the confidence of the classification (compared to the gradient Eq. 6.3) to determine the amount of adaptation. To avoid trivial solutions, additional regularization terms can be integrated e.g. the length of the contour or the size of the regions; however it was not implemented here.

The algorithm starts with an initial contour provided by the hypothesis $\mathcal{H}$, i.e.

$$\phi_{init}(\mathbf{x}) = \begin{cases} 1 & \text{if } H(\mathcal{H}(\mathbf{x})) = 0 \\ -1 & \text{if } H(\mathcal{H}(\mathbf{x})) = 1 \end{cases} \quad (6.12)$$

The iterative optimization of the level set function $\phi(\mathbf{x})$ consists of two steps. The first step keeps $\phi(\mathbf{x})$ fixed and minimizes the energy with respect to the prototypes $\mathcal{P}$ and relevance matrices Λ by standard LGMLVQ learning (Sec. 3.2) according to an intermediate hypothesis $\mathcal{H} = (1 - H(\phi(\mathbf{x})))$. In the second step, the level set function is adapted according to Eq. 6.11 using Heun's method (Chapra and Canale 1988), following the general form $y_{i+1} = y_i + \epsilon \cdot h$, with ϵ extrapolating from an old value y_i to a new value y_{i+1} with a step size h. Both steps are iteratively computed along the initial level set function until the function $\phi(\mathbf{x})$ converges or a

edge	cost w_e	for
$\{v,u\}$	Bound$(\mathcal{A}_v, \mathcal{A}_u)$	$\{v,q\} \in \mathcal{N}$
$\{v,v_s\}$	abs$(\mu(\mathcal{P}, \vec{\xi}(\mathbf{x})))$	$v \in \mathcal{V}, p \notin Fg \cup Bg$
	K	$v \in Fg$
	0	$v \in Bg$
$\{v,v_t\}$	abs$(\mu(\mathcal{P}, \vec{\xi}(\mathbf{x})))$	$v \in \mathcal{V}, v \notin Fg \cup Bg$
	0	$p \in Fg$
	K	$v \in Bg$

Table 6.1: *Definition of the weight cost according to (Boykov and Jolly 2001). The weight cost of the connection to unclassified pixels are defined by the classification, i.e. its confidence, the margin $\mu(\mathcal{P}, \vec{\xi}(\mathbf{x})) \in [0,1]$, Eq. 3.2. If confident initial labels are available they can be used as hard constraints. This is represented as a membership to foreground $v \in Fg$ or backgorund $v \in Bg$.*

maximum number of iterations is reached. In general, the level set function is updated close to the zero level set Ω^- determined by the regularized delta function $\delta(\phi, \tau) = \frac{1}{\pi} \cdot \frac{\tau}{\tau^2 + \phi^2}$.

6.3.2 Graph cuts formulation

Similar to the level set formulation the information from the GLVQ classifier is embedded in the graph cuts method. Here the region models e.g. histograms or Gaussian Mixture Models can be replaced by the response (or the confidence) of the pixel classifier. Following the general formulation (Eq. 6.6) consisting of two terms, this energy is defined as

$$E_{\text{gcI}}(\mathcal{A}) = \lambda \cdot \sum_{p \in \mathcal{V}} \text{Reg}(\mathcal{A}_v) + \sum_{v,u \in \mathcal{E}} \text{Bound}(\mathcal{A}_v, \mathcal{A}_u). \quad (6.13)$$

Here we modify the region term Reg$(\mathcal{A}_v)$ to determine the edge weights w_e according to Tab. 6.1. In this listing, the variable K represents a constant to define the maximum link strength that can be used as hard constraint. The margin according to Eq. 3.2 of the GLVQ classifier is used to define the region term, while the boundary term is kept as formulated in Eq. 6.7. Both terms are reflected in the definition of the graph that takes the region models and the neighborhood constraints into account. Finally the figure-ground segmentation is derived via standard min-cut/max-flow algorithm (Sec. 6.2.2) on the defined graph. Furthermore, similar to the iterative level set optimization, an iterative procedure can be formulated for graph cuts too. In the algorithm proposed by Rother et al. (Rother et al. 2004) the optimization is alternated between the region models and the graph cuts segmentation. The optimization starts with the initial hypothesis $\mathcal{H}$. Then the region models are adapted on the intermediate segmentations $\mathcal{A}$ until the algorithm converges or a maximum number of iterations is reached. Convergence can be measured by the number of pixels that changed their assignment from one to another iteration.

6.4 Simulations

6.4.1 Experimental setup

In this simulation we evaluate the performance of the proposed method and compare it to the state-of-the-art methods for figure-ground segmentation (i.e. level set (Weiler and Eggert 2007) methods and graph cuts (Boykov and Jolly 2001; Rother et al. 2004)). We apply the LGMLVQ algorithm separately and in combination with level set methods and graph cuts on the dataset introduced by Rother et al. (Rother et al. 2004). The dataset is public available and can be downloaded from the website of the authors[2]. The 50 images are collected with the purpose of object segmentation, i.e. consist of an object in front of a cluttered background, where the complexity of the object and background are very different within the dataset (compare to Fig. C.1). The images are of variable size and some of them are from the Berkeley Image Segmentation Benchmark Database (Martin et al. 2001). The images are selected to contain objects with no or little transparency. For each of the images three "trimap" are available (see examples in Fig. C.1), an "expert trimap", a "lasso trimap" and a "bounding box trimap". The expert trimap (Fig. 6.3) corresponds to a ground truth segmentation $\mathcal{A}^*$. This information was obtained by an user who traces the object outlines with a fine pen (Blake and Torr 2004). The "lasso trimap" and the "bounding box trimap" mimic several kinds of user-interaction and provide hypothetical foreground/background information $\mathcal{H}$.

Trimap setting vs. bimap setting For this benchmark the pixelwise ground truth information is provided (Fig. 6.4 (a)), which allows a quantification of the segmentation quality. Furthermore, for each image a gray-value image called "trimap" is available (here with two different setups Fig. 6.4 (b) and Fig. 6.4 (c)). Each trimap encodes the relationship of each pixel to foreground and background by one of four possible values $T = \{T_I = 0, T_B = 64, T_U = 128, T_F = 255\}$. This map mimics an user-interaction that can provide hints to the algorithm about the relation of each pixel to foreground T_F or background T_B, with the additional information of unknown status T_U or ignored regions T_I. In related work (Rother et al. 2004) foreground and background models are be learned on the known regions and used to classify

---
[2]http://research.microsoft.com/vision/cambridge/i3l/segmentation/GrabCut.htm

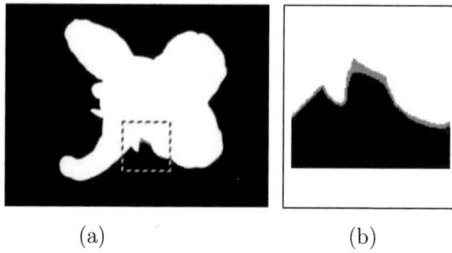

(a) (b)

Figure 6.3: *(a) Example of the ground truth information provided for the PBD dataset C.1. The ground truth was generated by a human tracing the outline of the object with a pen-tool (Blake and Torr 2004). (b) Focus on small boundary region of (a). The gray regions near the object boundary cover possibly mixed pixels from object and background and are excluded from the error measure E_B.*

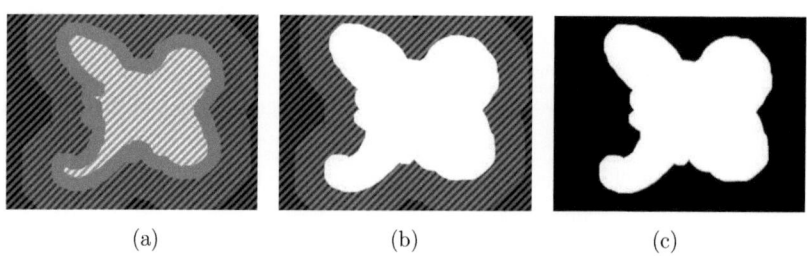

(a) (b) (c)

Figure 6.4: *Three different examples how the information of the trimap (see also the example in Fig. C.1) can be used to adapt the models and to constrain the optimization. (a) The complete information of the trimap is used. During the optimization the algorithm is not allowed to change the assignment of pixels in the regions T_F, T_B and T_I (blank regions vs. striped regions). (b) In contrast, a less constrained setup is used in (Rother et al. 2004). The regions T_F and T_U are used to adapt the foreground model and the pixels can be changed in their initial assignment. (c) The bimap setting poses no constraints on the algorithm. All pixels are used to adapt the models and can be changed in their assignment to foreground and background.*

the pixels of the unknown regions, without changing the assignment of pixels in the known parts. For the evaluation of the performance the unknown region is used. However for our work this scenario is not appropriate due to the fact that no user-interaction is available and no confident region classification to constrain the segmentation process can be given.

A more difficult setup can be used if only hypothetical foreground and background labels are provided (Fig. 6.4 (c)). These are used to train the model and no hard constraints are available for the algorithm. To derive a hypothesis to initialize the segmentation method (e.g. an initial level set function to start the iterative optimization) the concept of an unconstrained bimap is used. Here the hypothesis $\mathcal{H}$ can be derived by selecting T_I, T_B for background and T_F, T_U for foreground. Foreground and background models are learned on those hypothetical regions. In the evaluation step all pixels are allowed to change their initial assignment, which is critical to rate the efficiency of the algorithms according to the degree of information needed from the Trimap. The quality of the derived result can be evaluated according to the available ground truth information. As the algorithms are allowed to change the assignment of each pixel, in this case a pixelwise comparison is used.

$$E_B(\mathcal{A}, \mathcal{A}^*) = \frac{\sum_{\mathbf{x} \in \Omega} |\mathcal{A}(\mathbf{x}) - \mathcal{A}^*(\mathbf{x})|}{\sum_{\mathbf{x} \in \Omega} 1} \qquad (6.14)$$

6.4.2 Model parameter

Level-set parameters In general level set methods are sensitive to the choice of the parameters regarding the size or the properties of the image, e.g. compact objects vs. very articulated ones. For this reason we propose here an estimation of the level set parameters depending on the image data itself. For this, the properties of the hypothetical object shape are analyzed by means of the ratio of the two principle axes of the binary hypothesis $\mathcal{H}$. This is used to distinguish between compact and elongated target objects. Since elongated objects need a more flexible contour, the parameter ν (Eq. 6.11) was varied according to $\nu = \nu_0 + 3 \cdot (1 - \frac{1}{1+e^{(-10 \cdot (r^2 - 0.35))}})$ with an offset of $\nu_0 = 0.3$. Similarly a prior weighting of the position features was modified by $\frac{1}{1+e^{(-10 \cdot (r^2 - 0.35))}}$. Non-formally described, the ratio of the principle axes is put into a sigmoid function deciding, which object is elongated or not. In particular this prior weighting is important for metrics adaptation, since for elongated objects the learning dynamics concentrates on this property.

The method is applied in two different setups (Denecke et al. 2010). First, a single setup of parameters was used with an automatic parameter estimation for the contour parameter ν and the prior weighting of the position feature F_4 and F_5 (see Sec. 3.3). This is referred as to **Set 1** in the following section and Tab. 6.2. To improve the performance, a separate parameter search for parameter ν for each individual image was applied afterwards (referred as to **Set 2**). Additional parameters are also necessary for the GLVQ using metrics adaptation. In principle, prototype-based methods are confronted with a model selection problem, that is, to determine the appropriate number of prototypes for each class. We decided to apply the LGMLVQ method with an empirically determined setup of three prototypes for background and five prototypes for foreground. Similar as in Sec. 3.4.2.1 a regular sampling in the parameter space was used. Since the method is applied on single images the incremental procedure proposed in Chapter. 5 was not applied. This method can be integrated as well, but in this work we want to concentrate of the integration into the energy minimization techniques. For the first iteration the prototypes are initialized by means of k-means clustering without a particular feature weighting. The learning rates introduced in Sec. 3.2 were adopted from Sec. 3.4.2.1 with $\alpha = 0.05$ to adapt the prototypes $\mathcal{P}$ and $\beta = 0.005$ to adapt the relevance factors Λ_p. The number of adaptation steps of each iteration of the method was set to 10.000.

Graph cuts parameters For graph cuts (respectively Grab-cut (Rother et al. 2004)) the implementation provided by Justin Talbot was used, which is available online[3]. In order to achieve comparable conditions the parameters described in (Rother et al. 2004) are used. The number of components of the GMM or prototypes for GLVQ network was set to five, for foreground and background. The remaining graph cuts parameters are kept as proposed in (Rother et al. 2004), $\lambda = 50$ and $\beta = 1/(2\langle(\vec{\xi}_v - \vec{\xi}_u)^2\rangle)$ (see Sec. 6.2.2). Instead of GMM the LGMLVQ classifier is used. The parameterization is kept as before, i.e. $\alpha = 0.05$, $\beta = 0.005$, 10000 update steps for three prototypes for background and five prototypes for foreground. In contrast to the level set implementation no prior scaling of the position features was used, which might be beneficial as well, but would affect the comparability to the implementation using Gaussian Mixture Models.

6.4.3 Results

In this section the performance of our approach and the results of the other methods are reported, where we concentrate on the quantitative evaluation using the pixelwise error rate E_B. First of all, the hypothesis itself is compared to the ground truth data. This error provides the baseline for our evaluations and a successful approach should be capable to improve the match to the ground truth data. The results in Tab. 6.2 show our proposed models succeed regarding the baseline error of 7.72%. If the LGMLVQ model is used separately an error of 4.55% is achieved. Contrary to Chapter 3 and Chapter 4 in this setup a number of five prototypes for

---
[3] http://research.justintalbot.org/papers/GrabCut.zip

6.4. SIMULATIONS

Method	Error rate (avg. and std. dev.)	
	Baseline	
$\mathcal{H}$	07.72% ± 03.41	
LGMLVQ (B)	04.55% ± 03.10	
	Levelset	
Level-set (B)	- Histogram	04.98% ± 03.31
Condition (B)	- LGMLVQ, **Set 1**	02.41% ± 01.96
Condition (B)	- LGMLVQ, **Set 2**	01.73% ± 01.63
	Graph cuts	
Graph-Cut (B)	- GMM	05.86% ± 11.05
Graph-Cut (B)	- LGMLVQ	02.56% ± 02.47

Table 6.2: *Evaluation of the error rates of the proposed segmentation methods and state-of-the-art models on public benchmark data. To achieve comparability of the results, the error E_B is used in all conditions. The method for the region models is indicated as Histogram, GMM or LGMLVQ.*

foreground and background was used to achieve comparable results to the parameters used in the level set and graph cuts implementation.

Level set results In contrast to a descriptive level set implementation the integration of the region classifier is capable to improve the results compared to the individual application of metrics adaptation and level set methods with histograms (Weiler and Eggert 2007) (2.41% vs. 4.55% and 4.98%). These results are derived by using the parameter configuration **Set 1** with a fixed contour weighting ν. For level set methods the appropriate weighting of the contour contribution is crucial. Hence the contribution of this term is emphasized by using the parameter configuration **Set 2**. Sampling this curvature weight ν and taking the best results for each image, finally yields a significantly improved performance (1.73%).

Graph cuts results To our knowledge, the graph cuts segmentation (Boykov and Jolly 2001; Rother et al. 2004) currently achieves the best performance on this dataset. However those results are obtained by using the trimap setup (Sec. 6.4.1) and are not comparable to our work. Those results were derived making stronger assumptions and using more information provided by the trimap. Hard constraints were used to prevent that pixels of predefined image regions (e.g. T_F and T_B) can be changed in their assignment. In other words, the region to be classified is restricted to the unknown part T_U (Boykov and Jolly 2001) or at least the T_U together with T_F (Rother et al. 2004) (see Fig. 6.4). This can be used as starting point to compare the graph cuts implementation using the bimap setup. If the bimap is used instead of the trimap the segmentation error increases significantly (1.25% (Rother et al. 2004) to 5.86%[4]). Finally the results reported for the level set method can be verified on the graph cuts implementation. Using a LGMLVQ network instead of Gaussian Mixture Models allows a more robust handling of the bimap setting and improves the performance without changing the parameter setting (2.56% instead of 5.86%).

6.5 Discussion

The preceding results show that the integrated method of a discriminative classifier and the energy minimization techniques is capable to outperform the individual methods. Here we discuss the capabilities as well as the problems of these methods. In Fig. 6.5 three examples from **Set 1** of the level set implementation are shown together with the results of the graph cuts implementation using the bimap setting. Level set methods as well graph cuts allow the handling of non-compact objects. In other words, the object to segment can contain holes. For level set methods this capability is introduced by using region-based optimization presented in (Chan and Vese 2001). The usage of a feature classifier instead of pure region descriptors (the average value, histogram or Gaussian Mixture Model) also supports this capability. In contrast to a simple average of the region, the neural network model used in this work allows for the representation of heterogeneous colored foreground object and background. Furthermore, for both energy minimization techniques the initial hypothesis is not required to enclose the object of interest, which is not self-evident for contour-based methods. That is, the models are capable to include regions in the final segmentation that are not included in the hypothesis. This can be an advantage if the hypothesis is incomplete, but this is also a drawback if small shadows near the object boundary are consistently integrated in the hypothesis. Those shadows can be modeled with a separate prototype if the LGMLVQ method is used and are finally classified as foreground (partially this effect can be compensate and will be discussed for Fig. 6.6). The third example shows the capability of the method to handle similar colors in foreground and background. This capability is supported by the metrics adaptation used in GLVQ that enables a classification based on the most relevant features.

To visualize the difference between the pure feature classification on the basis of the LGMLVQ method and the integration in level set methods or graph cuts, we show some examples in Fig. 6.6. Here the results of the standard graph cuts are compared with the results of the pixelwise classification and the results of the graph cuts model using the LGMLVQ foreground

---

[4]In comparison to the results in (Denecke et al. 2009) another implementation was used, which explains the difference to the previously reported results.

6.5. DISCUSSION

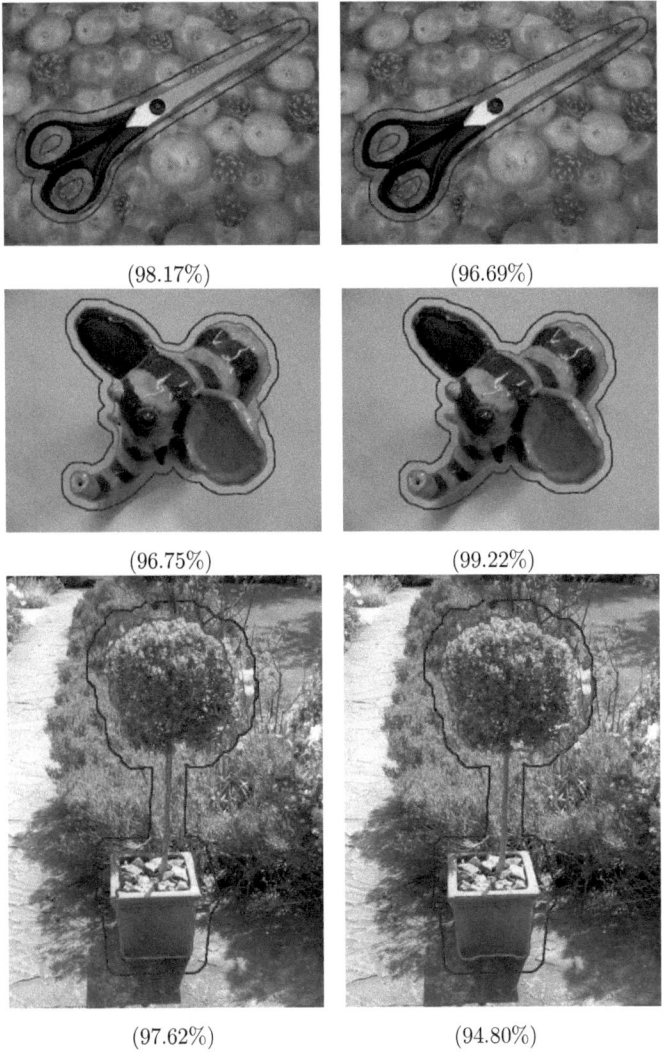

Figure 6.5: *Example results of the segmentation obtained by means of LGMVQ in combination with level set methods (left) and graph cuts (right). The blue lines are the outlines of the segmentation hypotheses, the red lines show the outlines of the segmentation results.*

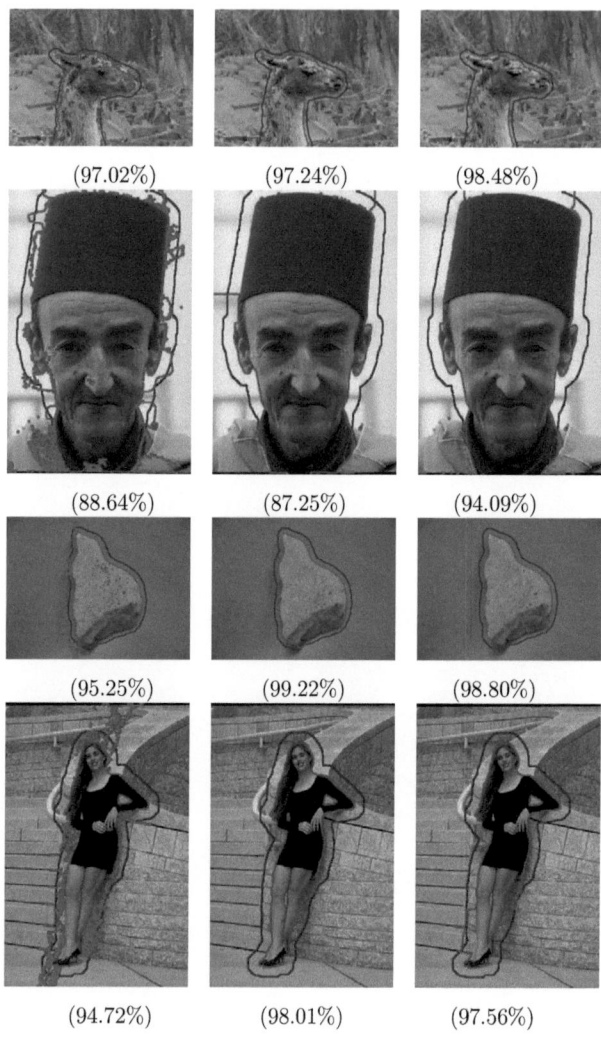

Figure 6.6: *Example results of graph cuts using Gaussian Mixtures Models (left column), the segmentation derived by LGMVQ (pixelwise foreground classification - middle column) and finally the right column shows results of graph cuts after a single iteration using the classification shown in the middle column. The blue lines are the outlines of the segmentation hypotheses, the red lines show the outlines of the segmentation results.*

classification. From these examples we can see several aspects. The influence of the contour term compared to the pixelwise classification, the effect of missing constraints for graph cuts, overfitting effect if too much prototypes are used and the influence of relevance determination. The first two images show examples of the benefit of integrating the LGMLVQ classifier and the energy minimization techniques. In these cases the classifier allows a robust classification also in the presence of the same colors in foreground and background. In an extreme case the classification only relies on the position and ignores the color. The remaining two examples visualize two problems of the LGMLVQ if no further region or contour constraints are used. In general prototype-based models are confronted with a model selection problem. As already stated in (Denecke et al. 2009) a fixed set of prototypes for the GLVQ method applied to all images of this particular dataset is not appropriate. A higher number of prototypes might increase the performance on complex scenes but leads to overfitting effects on the simpler scenes. In further work, incremental methods to estimate the model complexity can be used (Chapter 5). In the last example a particular problem of the metrics adaptation is shown. For elongated objects the optimization of the metrics in LGMLVQ can yield a large relevance for the first principle component in position space ($\mathcal{F}_{4,5}$). From the viewpoint of the importance of the classification this is correct, but a low weighting of the color features results in the misclassification of several pixels in this principle direction. Hence, for the level set method the prior weighting of the position features was introduced to compensate this effect as described in Sec. 6.4.2. The problem of misclassification due to overfitting and misleading relevance determination can be partially compensated by using additional region and contour constraints. Therefore the usage of those energy minimization techniques is beneficial to improve the foreground segmentation compared to the one-shot classification model. On the other hand the graph cuts method strongly relies on the confident trimap information and the performance is impaired if this is not available. The usage of the region classifier allows graph cuts to cope with this bimap setting.

6.6 Summary

In this chapter we addressed the task of hypothesis-based image segmentation by means of a neural network classifier in combination with state-of-the-art energy minimization techniques. The combination of the proposed algorithms produced competitive results on a common benchmark dataset and outperformed other established methods. Additionally we proposed a level set formulation, where a discriminative approach instead of descriptive region modeling was used to model the statistics of foreground and background. Similarly this approach was also implemented using the graph cuts method to show the benefit of metrics adaptation for region modeling. In both cases LGMLVQ integrates the concept of metrics adaptation to obtain a robust region classifier that can handle complex colored objects and is able to determine the relevant feature dimensions in order to discriminate between foreground and background. On the other hand level set methods and graph cuts impose further region constraints and a contour optimization to derive consistent segmentation. In particular this is an advantage compared to the application of metrics adaptation by its own.

Chapter 7

Conclusion

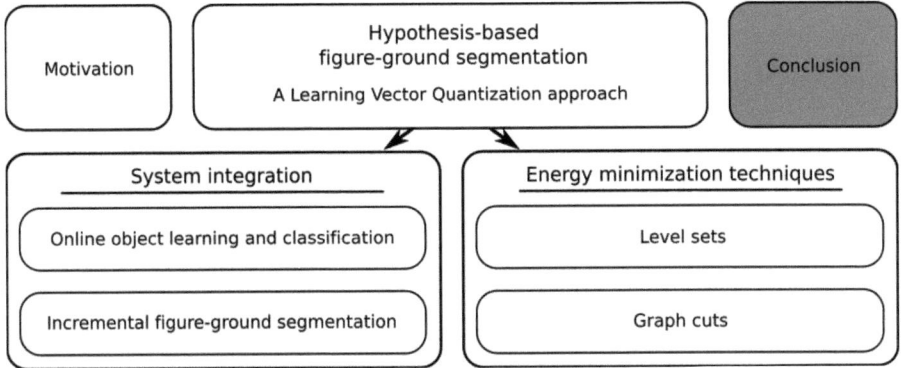

This thesis concerned the issue of automatic figure-ground segmentation of visual objects as basis for object learning and recognition. This took place in the context of integrated vision systems in a human-robot interaction scenario, where the purpose was to separate the object features from the background clutter to achieve invariance to the stimulus position in the scene. This scenario imposed several constraints on the work that makes it a challenging task. One of these constraints was for instance the necessity to segment previously unknown objects in a changing and unpredictable environment.

In this thesis we proposed a hypothesis-based approach to tackle this task and concerned an application of a Learning Vector Quantization (LVQ) algorithm. The main contribution of this thesis was to show that a neural network-based approach offers an efficient and real-time capable approach for the segmentation problem. In further work we addressed model specific problems like the network dimensionality and show that this approach is compatible with state-of-the-art energy minimization techniques in computer vision and image processing. In particular we showed that the discriminative approach can outperform established descriptive models in state-of-the-art techniques. In several chapters these properties and advantages of the model were analyzed and we gave extensive evaluations of the behavior and accuracy of the learning schemes for benchmark settings and real life applications.

With respect to the three initial research goals we can draw the following conclusions:

In Chapter 2 we proposed a hypothesis-based figure-ground segmentation, that is, an initial cue to segment a complex object (i.e. heterogeneous color, arbitrary pose) in front of cluttered and unconstrained background. To achieve this, a supervised Learning Vector Quantization approach was adopted and we focused on the relevant properties of the model, namely the robustness of the method to noisy initial segmentation hypothesis and the feature weighting ability. We investigated several adaptive metrics and evaluated their robustness to the noisy hypothesis and we could show that the manipulation of the metrics given a prototypical feature representation achieved a large gain in hypothesis refinement. From this work we can conclude that a neural networks-based approach can deal with this problem setting up to a significant degree of noise. Therefore, typical problems in hypothesis-based image segmentation like non-confident segmentation cues and similar colors in foreground and background can be efficiently handled.

A second major topic of our work was the successive integration of the method in complex vision systems. In Chapter 3 and 4 we addressed the real-world application of the method in the context of online-learning and real-time recognition. For this reason the figure-ground segmentation was evaluated as integral part of two visual recognition architectures. In these settings we verified the online capability of the method and its robust behavior on a large amount of data from dynamically changing scenes with background clutter. In the first step we showed that the model was capable to significantly improve the segmentation of the objects and that it could outperform state-of-the-art methods using simple segmentation cues. In contrast to other prototype-based approaches (Steil et al. 2007; Achanta et al. 2008) the proposed methods relaxed the a priori assumptions on object position and segment selection. In a next step the method was extended by an incremental learning scheme. Here we adopted a method to estimate the utility of the prototypes and showed, that the number of prototypes can be efficiently controlled by a small set of rules. In this setting we could show, that the incremental processing increases the stability of the method. In other words, the method was less dependent on the initialization of the prototypes and the variance of the results was significantly reduced. We can conclude that the proposed figure-ground segmentation scheme is a crucial step towards efficient visual learning in complex and cluttered environments. The proposed bottom-up processing yields a significant improvement of the recognition performance in online-learning and recognition scenarios.

Finally the integration of the proposed segmentation method into state-of-the-art energy minimization techniques was investigated in Chapter 6. This contribution extended the work of Chapter 3 in two aspects. Firstly those models facilitated an integration of concepts like neighboring image regions, compactness of the segmentation and shape among others. Secondly, level set methods as well as graph cuts allowed for an iterative processing that reduces of the dependence on the initial hypothesis.

We showed that the integration of those techniques yielded a mutual benefit compared to the state-of-the-art. Descriptive models are normally used when foreground and background were modeled independent of each other. The learning dynamics of Generalized Learning Vector Quantization that optimizes a classifier on the basis of the full available information could yield an advantage compared to the descriptive techniques. The neural networks-based approach on the other hand could take profit from the usage of further constraints imposed by the energy minimization techniques. Those constraints are image-based techniques and restrict the solution to spatially coherent results rather than pixelwise noisy classification. The methods itself were not evaluated in the context of real-time processing but offer several advantages and possibilities for future work.

7.1 Outlook

For future work three possible research directions are the extension towards the processing of spatio-temporal data, the competitive optimization of a multi-region segmentation and the ongoing relaxation of the human-robot interaction itself.

In graph cuts as well as level set methods the processing of video-data by the usage of tracking and prediction algorithms or a direct generalizing of the methods to spatio-temporal data are of current interest (Li et al. 2005; Wang et al. 2005). The GLVQ model is not constrained to the processing of two dimensional data and can be applied in these advanced models as well. In this thesis the real-time capability of the proposed graph cut and level set implementation was not addressed.

Another starting point for ongoing work is the fact that figure-ground segmentation is a special case of general image segmentation. Instead of a simplified model of foreground vs. background a possible goal for future research can be the usage of multiple competitive segmentation hypotheses. In comparison to unsupervised image segmentation the guidance by multiple hypotheses can restrict the amount of possible solutions towards task oriented results. Since the Learning Vector Quantization approach can handle an arbitrary number of classes the method is not restricted to a figure-ground segmentation problem. Therefore it is possible to treat the image segmentation as a three class optimization where the skin color detection provides an additional external hypothesis. In this case the skin color detection can be integrated as an additional cue, rather than a predefined processing step. Together with the depth hypothesis the representatives of three classes can be optimized in a competitive fashion. In case of such multi-hypotheses segmentation schemes the question occurs how to obtain the different hypotheses in an autonomous setting, which is an important step towards an unconstrained human-robot interaction. In this work unconstrained was defined as using image data with arbitrary background and a natural interaction i.e. the object are presented by hand. Nevertheless the scenario is still constrained in the sense that the concept of peri-personal space is an integration of external knowledge, which is also the case for the predefined integration of the skin-color detection. In other words, we designed the system to define what is to learn in an abstract way. To release those constraints the system has to determine by itself what is interesting for interaction and learning. In (Nordlund 1998) a model is proposed that analyses a 2-dimensional histogram in feature space to determine prominent depth blobs that correspond to the main parts of the scene. In the BRAVO-1 system the concept of proto-objects was already used (Sec. 4.4.2). This method is not restricted to a single proto-object and can serve as basis for more complex interactions.

To go a step further other concepts have to be used. The interaction of the figure-ground segmentation with an already acquired object representation is one of the most exciting topics. This work addressed the usage of available bottom-up cues and their integration with respect to an external hypothesis. The source of this hypothesis is not restricted to a particular model as pointed out in Sec. 2.2.2.2, but the problem of top-down segmentation is still an open one. The interaction of bottom-up and top-down processes is one possibility to develop a method that can be bootstrapped by an initial segmentation e.g. from depth, motion or proto-objects. The more information is available during learning the more this process can be enhanced. This concept is inspired from biological findings, such as on a psychophysical level Needham (Needham 2001; Needham and Baillargeon 1998) shows that prior experience affect the figure-ground segmentation capability of young infants. Furthermore there is more evidence for bottom-up and top-down interaction regarding figure-ground segmentation (Sec. 2.1.1.1). Nevertheless such top-down segmentation encounters several principle problems. In visual learning one goal is to build-up a high level object representation that is as invariant as possible from the sensory data. This allows recognition of entities despite of large visual variance like viewpoint, lightning conditions and context. To establish a relationship between the abstract high-level representation and the underlying sensory data is an unsolved problem.

Appendix A

Notation

According to the notation used in the related literature for Learning Vector Quantization, level set methods and graph cuts, a consistent notation used in all chapters was defined. Here the most important and commonly used symbols are listed. Further symbols that are used but not listed here, e.g. parameters of a particular algorithm, follow the notation of the cited literature and may be specific for each chapter. In general the vector, matrix and set notation is as follows:

- Calligraphic letters (e.g. $\mathcal{A}$) are used in two contexts. Firstly they denote sets. Secondly, they are used to denote special symbols like the binary segmentation $\mathcal{A}$ or the segmentation hypothesis $\mathcal{H}$.

- Vectors are always column vectors and are indicated by an arrow. A special case is the vector of coordinates that encode the position of a pixel. This vector is always denoted as $\mathbf{x}$ and is used as index for the image pixels.

- Matrices are denoted as uppercase Greek letters, e.g. the relevance matrix Λ. A special case is the image plane Ω to achieve consistence with the related literature for level set methods.

- Numbers are denoted as uppercase letters.

		Image data
M	-	Number of image features
Ω	-	Image plane
$\mathbf{x}$	-	Image position $\mathbf{x} := \{x, y\}, \mathbf{x} \in \Omega$
$\vec{\xi}(\mathbf{x})$	-	Feature vector at image position $\mathbf{x}$ with dimensionality M
$c[\cdot] \in \{0,1\}$	-	Binary label of a reference vector or feature vector
$\mathcal{F}$	-	Feature-map representation of an image
$\mathcal{D}$	-	Dataset representation of an image
$\mathcal{A}$	-	Binary segmentation mask
$\mathcal{A}^*$	-	Binary ground truth segmentation mask
$\mathcal{H}$	-	Binary segmentation hypothesis
$\mathcal{S}$	-	Binary skin color detection
T_F	-	Function for preprocessing of image data $\mathcal{F}$ (Sec. 4.2.1)
T_H	-	Function for preprocessing of hypothesis $\mathcal{H}$ (Sec. 4.2.3)
		Vector Quantization
N	-	Number of prototypes, i.e. the size of the artificial neural network
$\mathcal{P}$	-	Set of prototypes; Codebook
$\vec{w}_p$	-	Reference vector of prototype $p \in \mathcal{P}$
Λ	-	$M \times M$ matrix of relevance factors
d_J, d_K	-	Distances of a feature vector to best matching prototypes
		Energy minimization
$\phi(\mathbf{x})$	-	Level set function, dependent on the image position $\mathbf{x}$
$H(\cdot)$	-	Heavy-side function
$\mathcal{G}$	-	Graph representation of an image
$\mathcal{V}$	-	Set of nodes to define $\mathcal{G}$
$\mathcal{O}$	-	Subset of ordinary nodes in $\mathcal{V}$, nodes that correspond to pixels
v_s	-	Special "Source"-node
v_t	-	Special "Sink"-node
$\mathcal{E}$	-	Set of edges to define $\mathcal{G}$
$\mathcal{N}$	-	Subset of neighborhood edges in $\mathcal{E}$
$\mathcal{C}$	-	Subset of edges $\mathcal{C} \subset \mathcal{E}$ to define a cut on the graph $\mathcal{G}$

Appendix B

Abreviations

ASDF	-	Adaptive Scene-Dependent Filter
BASS	-	Brainlike Active Sensing System
BRAVO	-	Brain-like Representation Architecture for Visual Objects
EM	-	Expectation-Maximization
GLVQ	-	Generalized Learning Vector Quantization
GMM	-	Gaussian Mixture Model
IT	-	Inferior Temporal Cortex
LGN	-	Lateral Geniculate Nucleus
LOC	-	Lateral Occipital Complex
LVQ	-	Learning Vector Quantization
MT	-	Middle Temporal Cortex
NMF	-	Non-Negative Matrix Factorization
NNC	-	Nearest Neighbor Classifier
PCA	-	Principle Component Analysis
PDE	-	Partial Differential Equation
ROI	-	Region of Interest
SIFT	-	Scale-invariant Feature Transformation
SVM	-	Support Vector Machine
V1	-	Primary Visual Cortex
V4	-	Part of the visual cortex
WTM	-	Winner-Take-Most

APPENDIX B. ABREVIATIONS

Appendix C

Datasets

C.1 PBD: Public benchmark data

This public available benchmark dataset was presented in (Rother et al. 2004)) and can be downloaded from the website of the authors[1]. Twenty images are from the Berkeley Image Segmentation Benchmark Database (Martin et al. 2001). The 50 images are collected with the purpose of object segmentation, i.e. consist of an object in front of a cluttered background where the complexity of the object and background are very different within the dataset (Fig. C.1). The images are of variable size and are selected to contain objects with no or little transparency. For each of the images a ground truth segmentation and an initial region assignment is available. The ground truth segmentation was obtained by a user tracing the object outlines with fine pen (Blake and Torr 2004). In Sec. 6.4.1 we describe how the information of the initial region assignment is used.

C.2 HRIR25: HRI dataset of rendered objects

This dataset (Fig. C.2) was generated from a set of 25 realistic 3D objects (bottles, boxes, cars etc.) freely available from the internet. 3D rendering software was used to generate 700 images for each object while an arbitrary but continuous rotation was performed. The object-views are pasted in the center of a non-rendered scene (human in the background, hand near object, generated by tracking the view-centered hand in front of the camera system, see also Sec. 4.2). The purpose of this dataset is to mimic the real world data of the HRI50 and HRI126 datasets but with available ground truth segmentation. Additionally, the ground truth segmentation is used to generate artificial (noisy) segmentation hypotheses. The distortion mimics the noise

---

[1] http://research.microsoft.com/vision/cambridge/i3l/segmentation/GrabCut.htm

obtained from standard stereo depth algorithms. The method is described in Sec. 3.4.4. Due to copyright restrictions on the 3D-objects used for image rendering, the dataset cannot be published.

C.3   HRI50: Data from human-robot interaction

In our simulations we use the data from (Wersing et al. 2007) consisting of 50 natural, view centered objects with 300 training and 100 testing images without ground truth information (Fig. C.3). This image data was acquired using the active camera system described in 4.2 by tracking the object while a human presenter freely rotated the object in his hand. All scenes consist of a cluttered background and for the acquisition of training and test data different presenters were used. The dataset consists of images with the size of 144×144 pixels which are the cropped ROIs of the scene in the focus of attention. Additionally the depth information is also stored. Furthermore, for the experiments a skin color detection is performed, which is described in Sec. 4.2.3.

C.4   HRI126: Data from human-robot interaction

Compared to the HRI50, the HRI126 dataset (Fig. C.4) contains 126 objects each with 1200 views. The images are acquired under comparable conditions. That means, the objects were freely rotated in hand by two presenters in front of a cluttered background while the object is tracked by an active vision system (4.2). The images are also a cropped ROI from the scene and are scaled to a resolution of 144×144 pixels. The size of the ROI was determined based on depth information. This dataset was provided by Stephan Hasler (Hasler et al. 2009) and is more difficult than the HRI50 dataset. The reason is that in this set more objects belong to the same shape category and thus they look quite similar to each other. For example toy-ducks, toy-cars, cups, cans, tools, bottles, mobile phones, and animals, but also different fruits, vegetables and balls. The dataset was used for the experiments described in Sec. 4.4.2 and support the results on the HRI50 dataset (Sec. 4.4.1). For the experiments also a training/test separation is performed but not visualized here.

C.5   CAR: Data from car the detection scenario

Finally a dataset from a car detection scenario is used. The dataset consist of a short sequence of 35 images showing a car on the street. This dataset is in particular difficult due to the low color contrast between target object and background. Further the object size is significantly scaled during the sequence, which has to be normalized beforehand. The data shown in Fig. C.5 was generated by cropping the car with help of the provided ROI from the original scene together with some background. All cropped image are scaled to a standard size of 144 × 144 pixels, which compensates the different size of the object. The segmentation hypothesis is provided by the rectangular ROI as well.

Figure C.1: *Public benchmark dataset (Rother et al. 2004). The dataset consists of 50 images. For each image a pixelwise ground truth segmentation as well as a trimap that provides an initial region assignment is available.*

C.5. CAR: DATA FROM CAR THE DETECTION SCENARIO 123

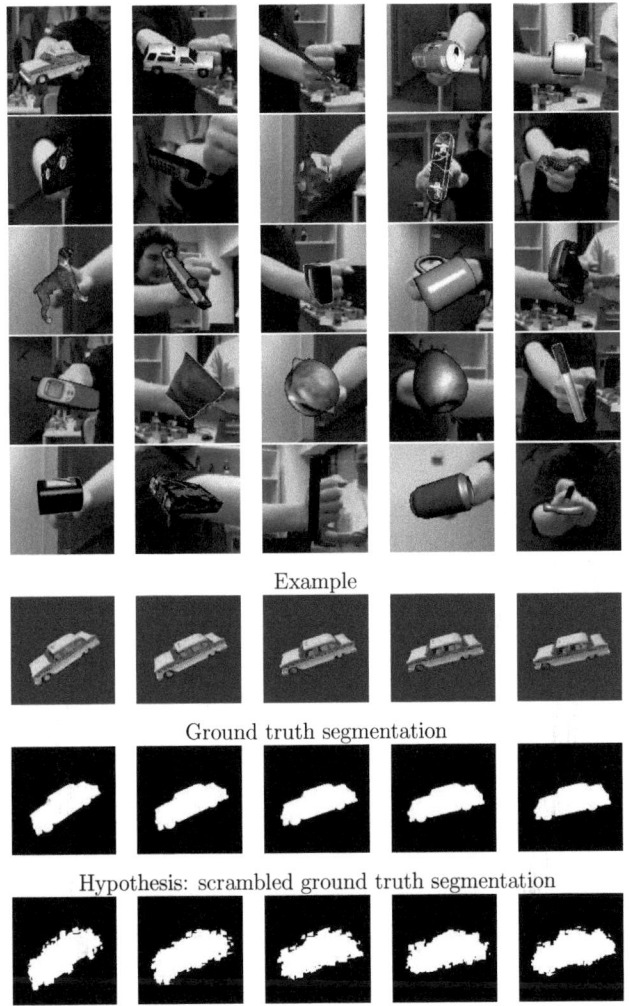

Figure C.2: *Overview of the HRI25 dataset: 25 rendered objects in front of a realistic background. Below an example from one of the image sequences is shown. The artificial hypothesis is generated from the ground truth, see Sec. 3.4.3.*

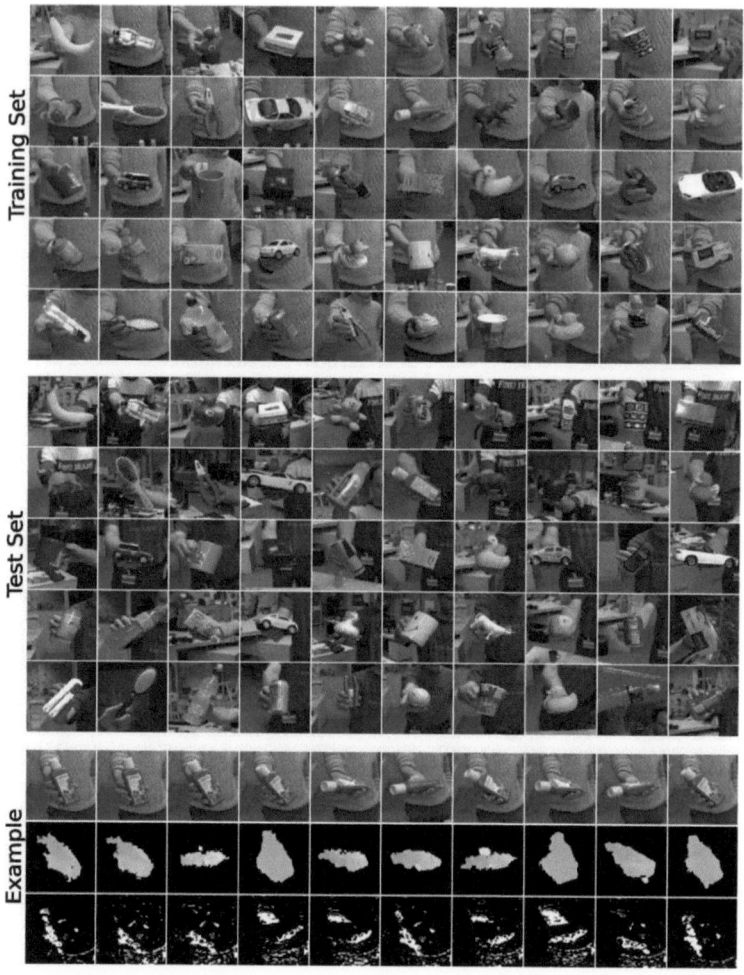

Figure C.3: *HRI50 dataset. The dataset consists of 50 view centered objects in front of a cluttered background. An initial segmentation cue can be derived from depth estimation and skin color detection (see Sec. 4.2.3).*

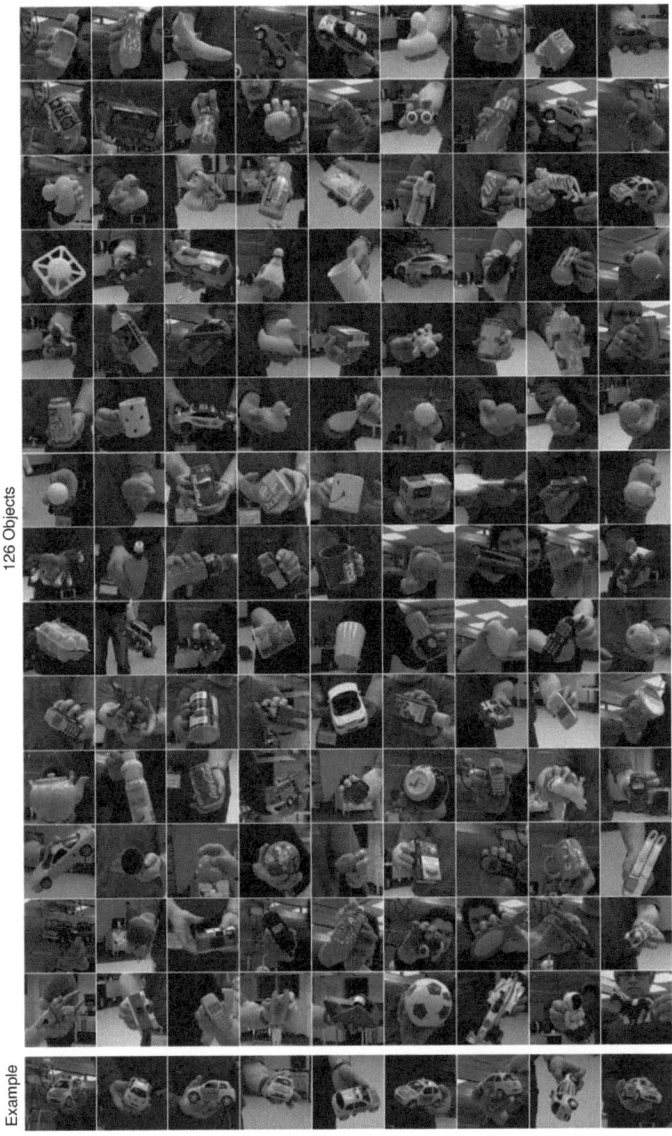

Figure C.4: *HRI126 dataset (Hasler 2010). The dataset consists of 50 view centered objects in front of a cluttered background. An initial segmentation cue can be derived from depth estimation and skin color detection (see Sec. 4.2.3).*

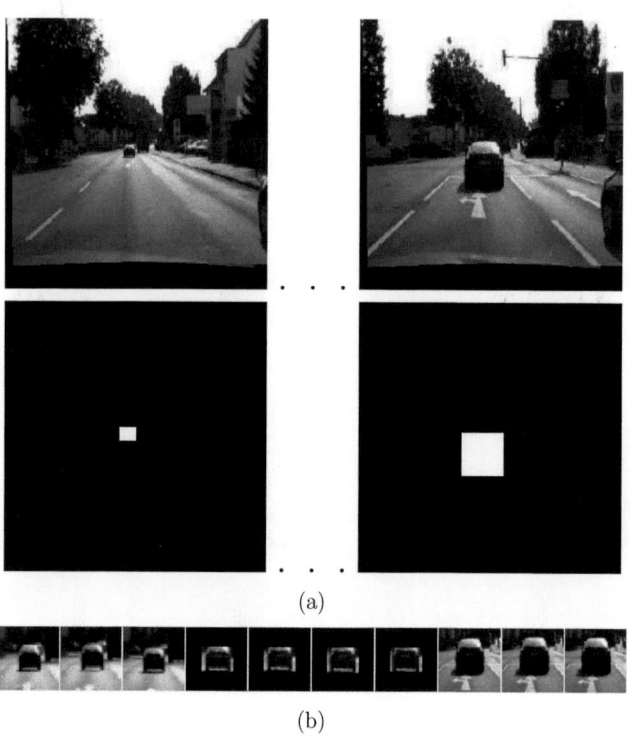

Figure C.5: *(a) First and last frame of the "car sequence" with corresponding ROI. Below the first and last three frames after preprocessing are shown together with some intermediate frames masked with the initial object hypothesis.*

Appendix D

Results

D.1 Image segmentation for CAR dataset

In this section the application of the LGMLVQ-algorithm is exemplified. The images are generated as part of the evaluation in Sec. 3.4.5 and show the overlay of the input image with the original non-displaced segmentation hypothesis (Fig. D.1) obtained by a car detection algorithm. The corresponding foreground classification results are shown in Fig. D.2, which are derived using **setup (a)**. In these images we can see that the algorithm is able to correctly classify the main object part. However due to a single prototype for each region in this setting, details like the window or number plate cannot be handled.

D.2 Image segmentation for HRI50 dataset

In addition to the results shown in Fig. D.2 on the following three figures (Fig. D.3, Fig. D.4, Fig. D.5) objects of the HRI50 (Fig. C.3) dataset are displayed. These results were obtained by the LGMLVQ algorithm (Sec. 3.3) and show the object view, the initial segmentation hypothesis (obtained from depth estimation and skin color detection, see Sec. 4.2.2) and finally the corresponding foreground classification. In all cases the segmentation results are more consistent with the main object parts compared to the initial hypothesis. Problems occur in some cases for small structures like tires and letters. The results are still noisy since no region-based concepts are used. Also simple postprocessing methods like a closing operation are not applied, since the impact on the final result is comparable low and such operation is not beneficial in all situations.

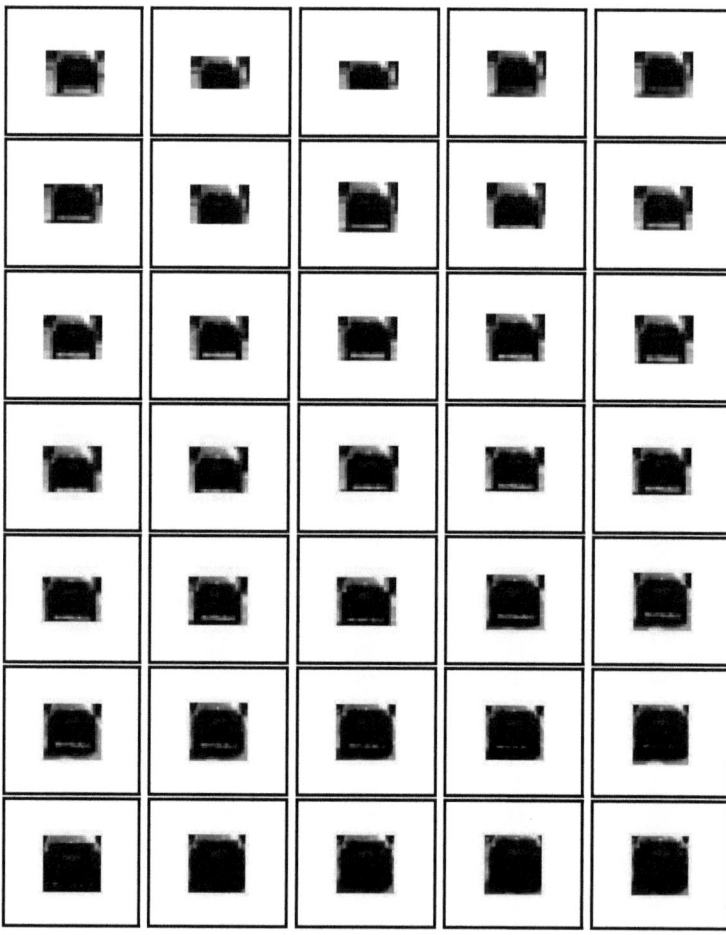

Figure D.1: *Image region covered by the initial segmentation hypothesis for CAR dataset.*

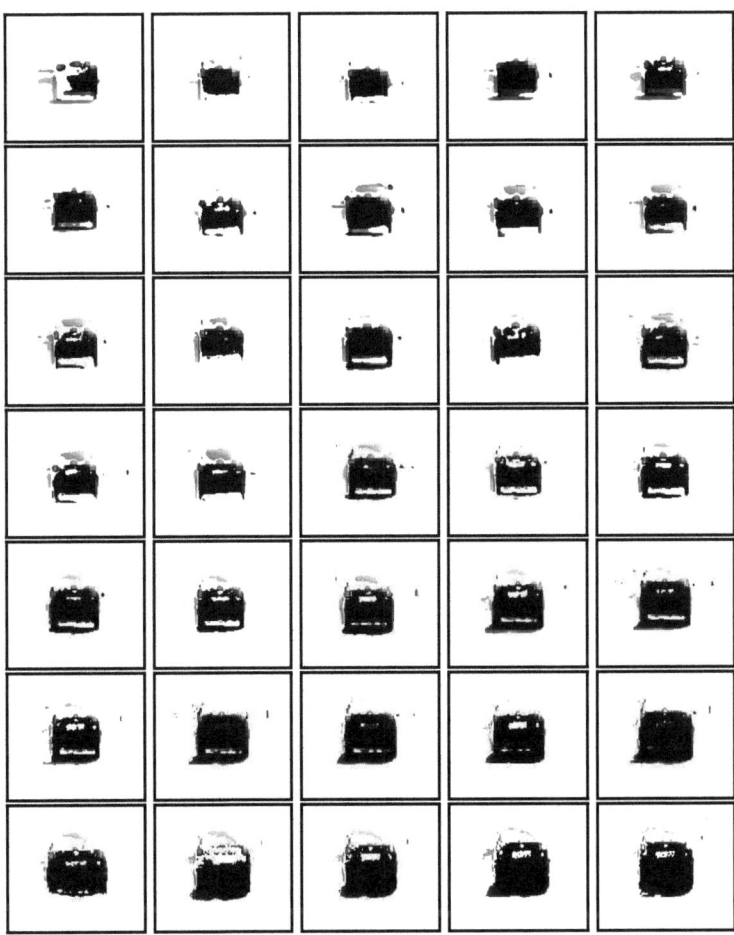

Figure D.2: *Foreground segmentation of the CAR dataset.*

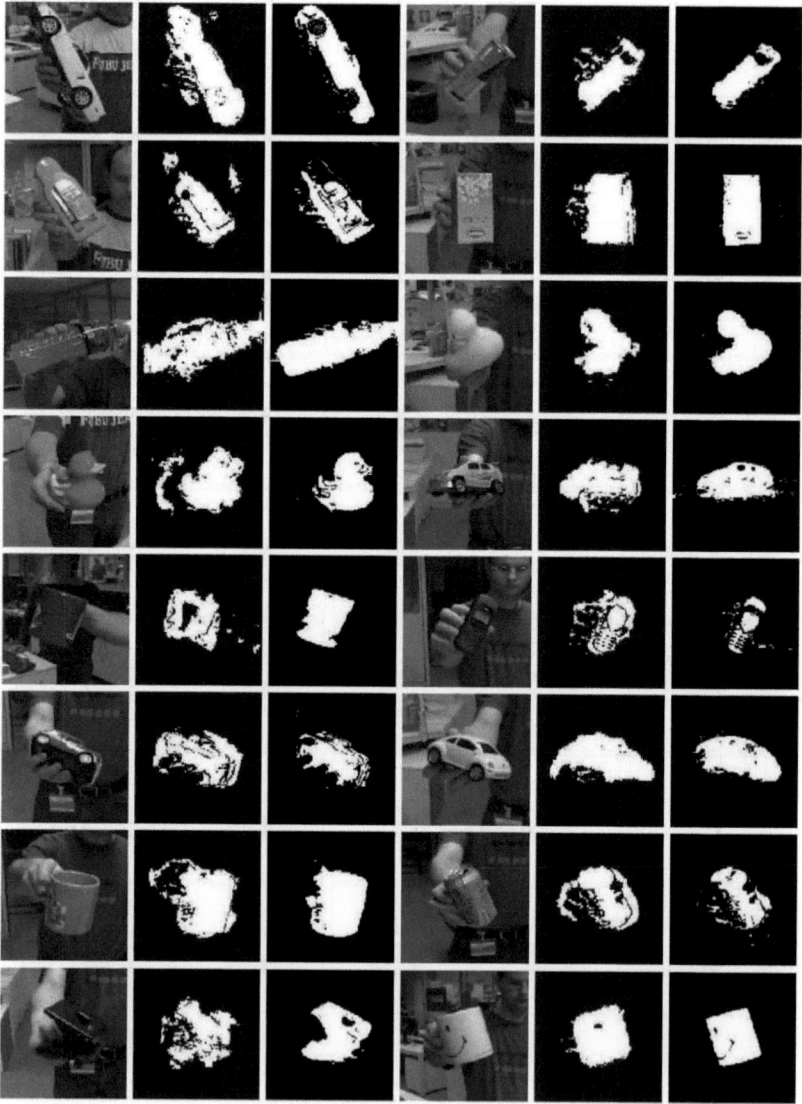

Figure D.3: *Examples of foreground segmentation of the HRI50 dataset - Part I.*

Figure D.4: *Examples of foreground segmentation of the HRI50 dataset - Part II.*

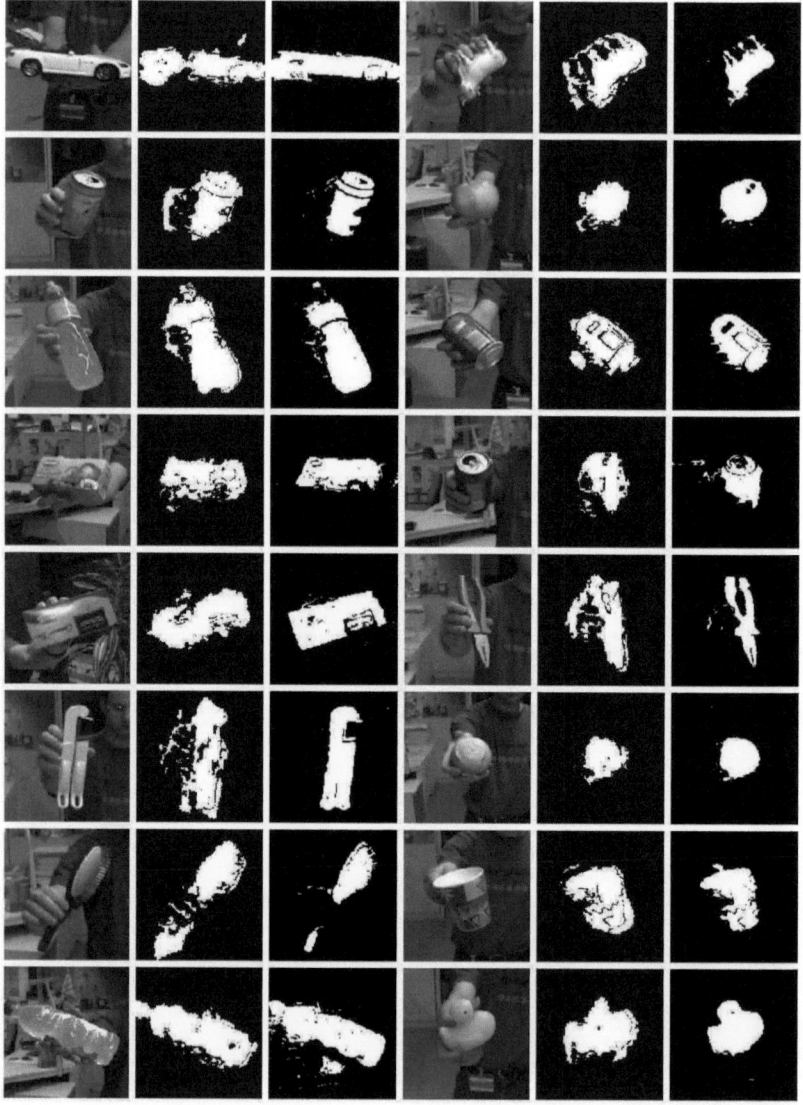

Figure D.5: *Examples of foreground segmentation of the HRI50 dataset - Part III.*

References

Achanta, R., F. Estrada, P. Wils, and S. Süsstrunk (2008). Salient region detection and segmentation. In *Proceedings of the 6th international conference on Computer vision systems*, pp. 66–75.

Altmann, C. F., A. Deubelius, and Z. Kourtzi (2004). Shape saliency modulates contextual processing in the human lateral occipital complex. *Journal of Cognitive Neuroscience 16*(5), 794–804.

Appelbaum, L. G., A. R. Wade, V. Y. Vildavski, M. W. Pettet, and A. M. Norcia (2006). Cue-invariant networks for figure and background processing in human visual cortex. *Journal of Neuroscience 26*(45), 11695–11708.

Arsenio, A. (2004a). Figure/ground segregation from human cues. In *Proceedings of the IEEE International Conference on Intelligent Robots and Systems (IROS)*, Volume 4, pp. 3244–3250.

Arsenio, A. M. (2004b). *Cognitive-Developmental Learning for a Humanoid Robot: A Caregiver's Gift*. Ph. D. thesis, M.I.T.

Arsenio, A. M. and P. M. Fitzpatrick (2005). Exploiting amodal cues for robot perception. *International Journal of Humanoid Robotics (IJHR) 2*, 125–143.

Bai, X. and G. Sapiro (2007). A geodesic framework for fast interactive image and video segmentation and matting. In *Proceedings of the IEEE International Conference on Computer Vision (ICCV)*, pp. 1–8.

Bai, X., J. Wang, D. Simons, and G. Sapiro (2009). Video snapcut: robust video object cutout using localized classifiers. *ACM Transactions on Graphics 28*(3), 1–11.

Bar, M., R. B. H. Tootell, D. L. Schacter, D. N. Greve, B. Fischl, J. D. Mendola, B. R. Rosen, and A. M. Dale (2001). Cortical mechanisms specific to explicit visual object recognition. *Neuron 29*(2), 529 – 535.

Bekel, H., I. Bax, G. Heidemann, and H. Ritter (2004). Adaptive computer vision: Online learning for object recognition. In *Proceedings of DAGM*, pp. 447–454.

Biehl, M., B. Hammer, P. Schneider, and T. Villmann (2009). Metric learning for prototype-based classification. In *Advances in Neural Information Paradigms*, Volume 247, pp. 183–199. Springer Studies in Computational Intelligence.

Bishop, C. M. (2007). *Pattern Recognition and Machine Learning (Information Science and Statistics)*. Springer.

Björkmann, M. and J.-O. Eklundh (2004). Attending, foveating and recognizing objects in real world scenes. *British Machine Vision Conference, Sep 2004*.

Blake, A., R. C. B. M. P. P. and P. Torr (2004). Interactive image segmentation using an adaptive GMMRF model. In *Proceedings of the European Conference on Computer Vision (ECCV)*.

Bolder, B., M. Dunn, M. Gienger, H. Janssen, H. Sugiura, and C. Goerick (2007). Visually guided whole body interaction. In *IEEE International Conference on Robotics and Automation (ICRA 2007)*.

Borenstein, E., E. Sharon, and S. Ullman (2004). Combining top-down and bottom-up segmentation. *Conference on Computer Vision and Pattern Recognition Workshop (CVPRW) 4*, 46.

Borenstein, E. and S. Ullman (2004). Learning to segment. In *Proceedings of the European Conference on Computer Vision (ECCV)*, pp. 315–328.

Boykov, Y. and G. Funka-Lea (2006). Graph cuts and efficient n-d image segmentation. *International Journal Computer Vision. 70*(2), 109–131.

Boykov, Y. and V. Kolmogorov (2001). An experimental comparison of min-cut/max-flow algorithms for energy minimization in vision. In *Proceedings of the Third International Workshop on Energy Minimization Methods in Computer Vision and Pattern Recognition*, pp. 359–374.

Boykov, Y., V. Kolmogorov, D. Cremers, and A. Delong (2006). An integral solution to surface evolution PDEs via geo-cuts. In *Proceedings of the European Conference on Computer Vision (ECCV)*, pp. 409–422.

Boykov, Y. Y. and M. P. Jolly (2001). Interactive graph cuts for optimal boundary & region segmentation of objects in n-d images. In *Proceedings of the IEEE International Conference on Computer Vision (ICCV)*, Volume 1, pp. 105–112.

Cadieu, C., M. Kouh, A. Pasupathy, C. E. Connor, M. Riesenhuber, and T. Poggio (2007). A Model of V4 Shape Selectivity and Invariance. *Journal of Neurophysiology 98*(3), 1733–1750.

Campbell, N., G. Vogiatzis, C. Hernández, and R. Cipolla (2010). Automatic 3D object segmentation in multiple views using volumetric graph-cuts. *Image and Vision Computing 28*(1), 14–25.

Carandini, M. (2006). What simple and complex cells compute. *Journal of Physiology 577*, 463–466.

Chan, T. and L. Vese (2001). Active contours without edges. *IEEE Transactions on Image Processing 10*(2), 266–277.

Chapra, S. and R. Canale (1988). *Numerical Methods for Engineers* (2nd ed.). McGraw-Hill.

Cheng, H.-D., X. Jiang, Y. Sun, and J. Wang (2001). Color image segmentation: advances and prospects. *Pattern Recognition 34*(12), 2259–2281.

Clemente, I. A. (2008). Investigation and implementation of a level-set based tracking system, incorporating contour prediction by means of different, collaborating prediction algorithms. Master's thesis, TU Darmstadt.

Comaniciu, D. and P. Meer (1997). Robust analysis of feature spaces: color image segmentation. In *Proceedings of IEEE Conference on Computer Vision and Pattern Recognition (CVPR)*, pp. 750.

Crammer, K., R. Gilad-Bachrach, A. Navot, and N. Tishby (2002). Margin analysis of the LVQ algorithm. In *Neural Information Processing Letters*, pp. 462–469.

Csurka, G., C. R. Dance, L. Fan, J. Willamowski, and C. Bray (2004). Visual categorization with bags of keypoints. In *Workshop on Statistical Learning in Computer Vision, ECCV*, pp. 1–22.

Denecke, A., I. A. Clemente, H. Wersing, J. Eggert, and J. J. Steil (2010). Figure-ground segmentation using metrics adaptation in levelset methods. In *Proceedings of the European Symposium on Artificial Neural Networks (ESANN)*, pp. 417–422.

Denecke, A., H. Wersing, J. J. Steil, and E. Körner (2008). Robust object segmentation by adaptive metrics in generalized LVQ. In *Proceedings of the European Symposium on Artificial Neural Networks (ESANN)*, pp. 319–324.

Denecke, A., H. Wersing, J. J. Steil, and E. Körner (2009). Incremental figure-ground segmentation using localized adaptive metrics in LVQ. In *Proceedings of 7th International Workshop on Self-Organizing Maps (WSOM)*, pp. 45–53.

Denecke, A., H. Wersing, J. J. Steil, and E. Körner (2009). Online figure-ground segmentation with adaptive metrics in generalized LVQ. *Neurocomputing 72*(7-9), 1470–1482.

DeValois, R. L., E. W. Yund, and N. Hepler (1982). The orientation and direction selectivity of cells in the macaque visual cortex. *Vision Research 22*, 531–544.

Duchenne, O. and J.-Y. Audibert (2006). Fast interactive segmentation using color and textural information. Technical report, CERTIS, ParisTech - Ecole des Ponts.

Duchenne, O., J.-Y. Audibert, R. Keriven, J. Ponce, and F. Ségonne (2008). Segmentation by transduction. In *Proceedings of IEEE Conference on Computer Vision and Pattern Recognition (CVPR)*, pp. 1–8.

Fergus, R., P. Perona, and A. Zisserman (2003). Object class recognition by unsupervised scale-invariant learning. In *Proceedings of IEEE Conference on Computer Vision and Pattern Recognition (CVPR)*, Volume 2, pp. 264–271.

Fitzpatrick, P. M. (2003). *From first contact to close encounters: a developmentally deep perceptual system for a humanoid robot*. Ph. D. thesis, Massachusetts Institute of Technology.

Ford, L. R. and D. R. Fulkerson (1962). *Flows in Networks*. Princeton University Press.

Friedland, G. (2006). *Adaptive Audio and Video Processsing for Electronic Chalkboard Lectures*. Ph. D. thesis, Department of Computer Science, Freie Universitaet Berlin.

Friedland, G., K. Jantz, T. Lenz, F. Wiesel, and R. Rojas (2007). Object cut and paste in images and videos. *International Journal of Semantic Computing 1*(2), 221–247.

Fritsch, J., S. Lang, M. Kleinehagenbrock, G. A. Fink, and G. Sagerer (2002). Improving adaptive skin color segmentation by incorporating results from face detection. In *IEEE International Workshop on Robot and Human Interactive Communication (ROMAN)*, pp. 337–343.

Fritzke, B. (1994). A growing neural gas network learns topologies. In *Neural Information Processing Letters*, pp. 625–632.

Fritzke, B. (1997). The LBG-U method for vector quantization – an improvement over LBG inspired from neural networks. *Neural Processing Letters 5*(1), 35–45.

Fu, K. and J. Mui (1981). A survey on image segmentation. *Pattern Recognition 13*(1), 3–16.

Fukushima, K. (1980). Neocognitron: A self-organizing neural network model for a mechanism of pattern recognition unaffected by shift in position. *Biological Cybernetics 36*, 193–202.

Gates, W. (2007). A robot in every home. *Scientific American 296*(1), 44–51.

Goerick, C., H. Wersing, I. Mikhailova, and M. Dunn (2005). Peripersonal space and object recognition for humanoids. In *Proceedings of the IEEE/RSJ International Conference on Humanoid Robots (Humanois 2005)*, pp. 387–392.

Goldberg, A. V. and R. E. Tarjan (1986). A new approach to the maximum flow problem. In *Proceedings of the eighteenth annual ACM symposium on Theory of computing (STOC)*, pp. 136–146.

Goodale, M. A. and A. D. Milner (1992). Separate pathways for perception and action. *Trends in Neuroscience 15*, 20–25.

Goodale, M. A. and D. A. Westwood (2004, April). An evolving view of duplex vision: separate but interacting cortical pathways for perception and action. *Current Opinion in Neurobiology 14*(2), 203–211.

Grauman, K. and T. Darrell (2007). The pyramid match kernel: Efficient learning with sets of features. *Journal of Machine Learning Research 8*, 725–760.

Greig, D. M., B. T. Porteous, and A. H. Seheult (1989). Exact maximum a posteriori estimation for binary images. *Journal of the Royal Statistical Society. Series B (Methodological)*, 271–279.

Grill-Spector, K. (2003). The neural basis of object perception. *Current Opinion in Neurobiology 13*(2), 159–66.

Grill-Spector, K., Z. Kourtzi, and N. Kanwisher (2001). The lateral occipital complex and its role in object recognition. *Vision Research 41*, 1409–1422.

Grill-Spector, K., T. Kushnir, T. Hendler, and R. Malach (2000). The dynamics of object-selective activation correlate with recognition performance in humans. *Nature Neuroscience 3*, 837–843.

Guan, J. and G. Qiu (2006). Interactive image segmentation using optimization with statistical priors. In *International Workshop on The Representation and Use of Prior Knowledge in Vision*.

Hamker, F. H. (2001). Life-long learning cell structures —continuously learning without catastrophic interference. *Neural Networks 14*(4-5), 551–573.

Hamker, F. H. (2002). How does the ventral pathway contribute to spatial attention and the planning of eye movements? In *Dynamic Perception*, pp. 83–88.

Hammer, B. and T. Villmann (2002). Generalized relevance learning vector quantization. *Neural Networks 15*(8-9), 1059–1068.

Hanbury, A. (2008). How do superpixels affect image segmentation? In *Proceedings of the 13th Iberoamerican congress on Pattern Recognition (CIARP)*, pp. 178–186.

Hasler, S. (2010). *Learning Features for Robust Object Recognition*. Ph. D. thesis, Bielefeld University, Faculty of Technology.

Hasler, S., H. Wersing, S. Kirstein, and E. Körner (2009). Large-scale real-time object identification based on analytic features. In *Proceedings of the 19th International Conference on Artificial Neural Networks (ICANN)*, pp. 663–672.

Hasler, S., H. Wersing, and E. Körner (2007a). Combining reconstruction and discrimination with class-specific sparse coding. *Neural Computation 19*(7), 1897–1918.

Hasler, S., H. Wersing, and E. Körner (2007b). A comparison of features in parts-based object recognition hierarchies. In *Artificial Neural Networks (ICANN)*, LNCS, pp. 210–219.

Howard, H. (2004). *Neuromimetic Semantics: Coordination, Quantification, and Collective Predicates*. Elsevier.

Hubel, D. H. and T. N. Wiesel (1962). Receptive fields, binocular interaction and functional architecture in the cat's visual cortex. *Journal of Physiology 160*(1), 106–154.

Hubel, D. H. and T. N. Wiesel (1965). Receptive fields and functional architecture in two nonstriate visual areas (18 and 19) of the cat. *Journal Neurophysiology 28*(2), 229–289.

Itti, L. (2000). *Models of Bottom-Up and Top-Down Visual Attention*. Phd thesis, California Institute of Technology, Pasadena, California.

Itti, L. and P. Baldi (2005). A principled approach to detecting surprising events in video. In *Proceedings of IEEE Conference on Computer Vision and Pattern Recognition (CVPR)*, pp. 631–637.

Itti, L., C. Koch, and E. Niebur (1998). A model of saliency-based visual attention for rapid scene analysis. *IEEE Transactions on Pattern Analysis and Machine Intelligence 20*(11), 1254–1259.

Jirayusakul, A. and S. Auwatanamongkol (2007). A supervised growing neural gas algorithm for cluster analysis. *International Journal on Hybrid Intelligent Systems 4*(4), 217–229.

Jones, J. P. and L. A. Palmer (1987). An evaluation of the two-dimensional Gabor filter model of simple receptive fields in cat striate cortex. *Journal Neurophysiology 58*(6), 1233–1258.

Kanwisher, N., M. M. Chun, J. McDermott, and L. P. J. (1996). Functional imaging of human visual recognition. *Cognitive Brain Research 5*(1-2), 55–67.

Kass, M., A. Witkin, and D. Terzopoulos (1988). Snakes: Active contour models. *International Journal of Computer Vision 1*(4), 321–331.

Kim, H., E. Murphy-Chutorian, and J. Triesch (2006). Semi-autonomous learning of objects. In *Proceedings of the Conference on Computer Vision and Pattern Recognition Workshop (CVPRW)*, pp. 145.

Kimchi, R. and M. A. Peterson (2008). Figure-ground segmentation can occur without attention. *Journal of Vision 8*(6).

Kinnunen, T., J.-K. Kamarainen, L. Lensu, and H. Kälviäinen (2009). Bag-of-features codebook generation by self-organisation. In *Proceedings of the 7th International Workshop on Advances in Self-Organizing Maps (WSOM)*, pp. 124–132.

Kirstein, S. (2010). *Interactive and Life-Long Learning for Identification and Categorization Tasks*. Ph. D. thesis, Technischen Universität Ilmenau.

Kirstein, S., H. Wersing, and E. Körner (2005a). Online learning for object recognition with a hierarchical visual cortex model. In *Artifical Neural Networks: Biological Inspiration (ICANN)*, pp. 487–492.

Kirstein, S., H. Wersing, and E. Körner (2005b). Rapid online learning of objects in a biologically motivated recognition architecture. In *DAGM-Symposium 2005*, pp. 301–308.

Kirstein, S., H. Wersing, and E. Körner (2008). A biologically motivated visual memory architecture for online learning of objects. *Neural Networks 1*, 65–77.

Koffka, K. (1935). Principles of gestalt psychology. New York: Harcourt, Brace & Co.

Kohonen, T., M. R. Schroeder, and T. S. Huang (Eds.) (2001). *Self-Organizing Maps*. Springer-Verlag New York, Inc.

Kolmogorov, V. and R. Zabih (2002). What energy functions can be minimized via graph cuts? In *Proceedings of the 7th European Conference on Computer Vision-Part III*, pp. 65–81.

Koshino, H., P. A. Carpenter, T. A. Keller, and M. A. Just (2005, March). Interactions between the dorsal and the ventral pathways in mental rotation: An fMRI study. *Cognitive, Affective, & Behavioral Neuroscience 5*(1), 54–66.

Kovács, I. and B. Julesz (1993). A closed curve is much more than an incomplete one: Effect of closure in figure-ground segmentation. In *Proceedings of the National Academy of Sciences (PNAS)*, Volume 90, pp. 7495–7497.

Kumar, M. P., P. H. S. Torr, and A. Zisserman (2005). OBJ CUT. In *Proceedings of IEEE Conference on Computer Vision and Pattern Recognition (CVPR)*, Volume 1, pp. 18–25.

Lamme (1995). The neurophysiology of figure-ground segregation in primary visual cortex. *Journal of Neuroscience 15*, 1605–1615.

Lamme, V. A. F., K. Zipser, and H. Spekreijse (1998). Figure-ground activity in primary visual cortex is suppressed by anesthesia. *Proceedings of the National Academy of Sciences (PNAS) 95*(6), 3263–3268.

Lee, D. D. and H. S. Seung (1999). Learning the parts of objects by non-negative matrix factorization. *Nature* 401(6755), 788–791.

Leibe, B., A. Leonardis, and B. Schiele (2007). Robust object detection with interleaved categorization and segmentation. *International Journal of Computer Vision* 77, 259–289.

Leibe, B. and B. Schiele (2003). Interleaved object categorization and segmentation. In *British Machine Vision Conference (BMVC)*, pp. 759–768.

Lempitsky, V., P. Kohli, C. Rother, and T. Sharp (2009). Image segmentation with a bounding box prior. In *Proceedings of the IEEE International Conference on Computer Vision (ICCV)*, pp. 277–284.

Lerner, Y., Hendler, and R. Malach (2002). Object-completion effects in the human lateral occipital complex. *Cerebral Cortex* 12(2), 163–177.

Li, P. and L. Xiao (2009). Histogram-based partial differential equation for object tracking. In *Proceedings of the IEEE International Conference on Advances in Pattern Recognition*, Volume 0, pp. 286–289.

Li, Y., J. Sun, and H.-Y. Shum (2005). Video object cut and paste. *ACM Transactions on Graphics* 24(3), 595–600.

Liu, W. and N. Zheng (2004). Non-negative matrix factorization based methods for object recognition. *Pattern Recognition Letters* 25(8), 893–897.

Lloyd, S. (1982). Least squares quantization in PCM. *IEEE Transactions on Information Theory* 28(2), 129–137.

Loos, H. S. and C. von der Malsburg (2002). 1-click learning of object models for recognition. *Biologically Motivated Computer Vision* 2525, 185–201.

Lowe, D. G. (2004). Distinctive image features from scale-invariant keypoints. *International Journal Computer Vision* 60(2), 91–110.

Lucchese, L. and S. Mitra (2001). Color image segmentation: A state-of-the-art survey. In *Proceedings of the Indian National Science Academy (INSAA)*, Volume 67A, pp. 207–221.

Macqueen, J. B. (1967). Some methods of classification and analysis of multivariate observations. In *Proceedings of the Fifth Berkeley Symposium on Mathematical Statistics and Probability*, pp. 281–297.

Malach, R., J. B. Reppas, R. R. Benson, K. K. Kwong, H. Jiang, W. A. Kennedy, P. J. Ledden, T. J. Brady, B. R. Rosen, and R. B. Tootell (1995). Object-related activity revealed by functional magnetic resonance imaging in human occipital cortex. In *Proceedings of the National Academy of Sciences (PNAS)*.

Martin, D., C. Fowlkes, D. Tal, and J. Malik (2001, July). A database of human segmented natural images and its application to evaluating segmentation algorithms and measuring ecological statistics. In *Proceedings of the IEEE International Conference on Computer Vision (ICCV)*, Volume 2, pp. 416–423.

McMail, T. C. (2009). Next-generation research and breakthrough innovation. *Computing in Science and Engineering 11*, 76–84.

Mel, B. W. (1997). Seemore: combining color, shape, and texture histogramming in a neurally inspired approach to visual object recognition. *Neural Computation 9*(4), 777–804.

Mishkin, M., L. G. Ungerleider, and K. A. Macko (1983). Object vision and spatial vision: two cortical pathways. *Trends in Neurosciences 6*, 414 – 417.

Mumford, D. and J. Shah (1989). Optimal approximations by piecewise smooth functions and associated variational problems. *Communications on Pure and Applied Mathematics 42*(5), 577–685.

Mutch, J. and D. G. Lowe (2006). Multiclass object recognition with sparse, localized features. In *Proceedings of IEEE Conference on Computer Vision and Pattern Recognition (CVPR)*, pp. 11–18.

Needham, A. (2001). Object recognition and object segregation in 4.5-month-old infants. *Journal of Experimental Child Psychology 78*, 3–22(20).

Needham, A. and R. Baillargeon (1998). Effects of prior experience on 4.5-month old infants' object segregation. *Infant Behavior and Development 21*, 1–24(24).

Ning, J., L. Zhang, D. Zhang, and C. Wu (2010). Interactive image segmentation by maximal similarity based region merging. *Pattern Recognition 43*(2), 445–456.

Nordlund, P. (1998). *Figure-Ground Segmentation Using Multiple Cues*. Phd thesis, Stockholms Universitet.

Olshausen, B. and D. Field (1997). Sparse coding with an overcomplete basis set: A strategy employed by V1? *Vision Research 37*, 3311–3325.

Osher, S. and R. Fedkiw (2002). *Level Set Methods and Dynamic Implicit Surfaces*. Springer.

Osher, S. and J. Sethian (1988). Fronts propagating with curvature-dependent speed: Algorithms based on Hamilton-Jacobi formulations. *Journal of Computational Physics 79*, 12–49.

Pal, N. and S. Pal (1993). A review on image segmentation techniques. *Pattern Recognition 26*(9), 1277–1294.

Palmer, S. E. (1999). *Vision science : photons to phenomenology*. MIT Press.

Pasupathy, A. and C. E. Connor (2002). Population coding of shape in area V4. *Nature Neuroscience 5*(12), 1332–1338.

Peterson, M. A. (1994). Object recognition processes can and do operate before figure-ground organization. *Current Directions in Psychological Science 3*, 105–111.

Peterson, M. A. (1999). Organization, segregation and object recognition. *Intellectica 28*, 37–51.

Pomierski, T. and H.-M. Gross (1996). Biological neural architecture for chromatic adaptation resulting in constant color sensations. In *Proceedings of the IEEE International Conference on Neural Networks (ICNN)*, pp. 734–739.

Price, B. L., B. Morse, and S. Cohen (2010). Geodesic graph cut for interactive image segmentation. In *Proceedings of IEEE Conference on Computer Vision and Pattern Recognition (CVPR)*, pp. 3161–3168.

Qiu, F. T. and R. von der Heydt (2005). Figure and ground in the visual cortex: V2 combines stereoscopic cues with gestalt rules. *Neuron 47*(1), 155–166.

Ren, X. and J. Malik (2003). Learning a classification model for segmentation. In *Proceedings of the IEEE International Conference on Computer Vision (ICCV)*, pp. 10.

Riesenhuber, M. and T. Poggio (1999). Hierarchical models of object recognition in the cortex. *Nature Neuroscience 2*(11), 1019–1025.

Rock, I. (1983). *The Logic of Perception.* Cambridge, Massachusetts: M.I.T. Press.

Rother, C., V. Kolmogorov, and A. Blake (2004). GrabCut: interactive foreground extraction using iterated graph cuts. *ACM Transactions on Graphics 23*(3), 309–314.

Rubin, E. (1921). Visuell wahrgenommene figuren. Kobenhaven: Glydenalske boghandel.

Rubin, E. (1958). Figure and ground. In D. Beardslee and M. Wertheimer (Eds.), *Readings in perception*, pp. 194–203. Princeton. Original work published 1915.

Sakai, K. and H. Nishimura (2006). Surrounding suppression and facilitation in the determination of border ownership. *Journal of Cognitive Neuroscience 18*, 562–579.

Sato, A. and K. Yamada (1995). Generalized learning vector quantization. In *Advances in Neural Information Processing Systems*, Volume 7, pp. 423–429.

Schleif, F. M., B. Hammer, and T. Villmann (2007). Margin-based active learning for LVQ networks. *Neurocomputing 70*(7-9), 1215–1224.

Schlesinger, M. and R. Limongi (2005). Towards a what-and-where model of infants' object representations. In *Proceedings of the AAAI Spring Symposium on Developmental Robotics*.

REFERENCES

Schmüdderich, J. M. (2010). *Multimodal Learning of Grounded Concepts in Embodied Systems*. Ph. D. thesis, Bielefeld University, Faculty of Technology.

Schneider, P., M. Biehl, and B. Hammer (2007). Relevance matrices in LVQ. In *Proceedings of the European Symposium on Artificial Neural Networks (ESANN)*, pp. 37–42.

Schneider, P., M. Biehl, and B. Hammer (2009a). Adaptive relevance matrices in learning vector quantization. *Neural Computation 21*(12), 3532–3561.

Schneider, P., M. Biehl, and B. Hammer (2009b). Distance learning in discriminative vector quantization. *Neural Computation 21*(10), 2942–2969.

Shi, J. and J. Malik (2000). Normalized cuts and image segmentation. *IEEE Transactions on Pattern Analysis and Machine Intelligence 22*(8), 888–905.

Steil, J. J., M. Götting, H. Wersing, E. Körner, and H. Ritter (2007). Adaptive scene-dependent filters for segmentation and online learning of visual objects. *Neurocomputing 70*(7-9), 1235–1246.

Sugihara, T., Y. Tsuji, , and K. Sakai (2007). Border-ownership-dependent tilt aftereffect in incomplete figures. *Journal of Optical Society of America A 24*, 18–24.

Sun, J., W. Zhang, X. Tang, and H. Shum (2006). Background Cut. In *Proceedings of the European Conference on Computer Vision (ECCV)*, pp. II: 628–641.

Swain, M. J. and D. H. Ballard (1991). Color indexing. *International Journal of Computer Vision 7*, 11–32.

Tanaka, K. (2003). Columns for Complex Visual Object Features in the Inferotemporal Cortex: Clustering of Cells with Similar but Slightly Different Stimulus Selectivities. *Cerebral Cortex 13*(1), 90–99.

Turk, M. A. and A. P. Pentland (1991). Face recognition using eigenfaces. In *Proceedings of IEEE Conference on Computer Vision and Pattern Recognition (CVPR)*, pp. 586–591.

Ullman, S., M. Vidal-Naquet, and E. Sali (2002). Visual features of intermediate complexity and their use in classification. *Nature Neuroscience 5*(7), 682–687.

Unger, M., T. Pock, and H. Bischof (2008). Continuous globally optimal image segmentation with local constraints. Computer Vision Winter Workshop.

Ungerleider, L. and J. Haxby (1994). What and where in the human brain. *Current Opinion in Neurobiology 4*(2), 157–165.

VanRullen, R. (2003). Visual saliency and spike timing in the ventral visual pathway. *Journal of Physiology 97*(2-3), 365–377.

Vecera, S. P. and R. C. O'Reilly (1998). Figure-ground organization and object recognition processes: An interactive account. *Journal of Experimental Psychology 24*(2), 441–462.

Vergés Llahí, J. (2005). *Color Constancy and Image Segmentation Techniques for Applications to Mobile Robotics.* Ph. D. thesis, University of Catalonia (UPC).

Vicente, S., V. Kolmogorov, and C. Rother (2009). Joint optimization of segmentation and appearance models. In *Proceedings of the IEEE International Conference on Computer Vision (ICCV)*, pp. 755–762.

von der Heydt, R., T. Macuda, and F. Qiu (2005). Border-ownership-dependent tilt aftereffect. *Journal of Optical Society of America A 22*(10), 2222–2229.

Voorhies, R. C., L. Elazary, and L. Itti (2010). Application of a bottom-up visual surprise model for event detection in dynamic natural scenes. *Journal of Vision 10*(7), 215.

Walther, D. (2006). *Interactions of Visual Attention and Object Recognition: Computational Modeling, Algorithms, and Psychophysics.* Phd thesis, California Institute of Technology, Pasadena, California.

Walther, D., U. Rutishauser, C. Koch, and P. Perona (2005). Selective visual attention enables learning and recognition of multiple objects in cluttered scenes. *Computer Vision and Image Understanding 100*(1-2), 41–63.

Wang, J. (2007). Discriminative gaussian mixtures for interactive image segmentation. In *Proceedings of the International Conference on Acoustics, Speech, and Signal Processing (ICASSP)*, pp. 601–604.

Wang, J., P. Bhat, R. A. Colburn, M. Agrawala, and M. F. Cohen (2005). Interactive video cutout. *ACM Transactions on Graphics 24*(3), 585–594.

Wang, J., T. Zhou, M. Qiu, A. Du, K. Cai, Z. Wang, C. Zhou, M. Meng, Y. Zhuo, S. Fan, and L. Chen (1999). Relationship between ventral stream for object vision and dorsal stream for spatial vision: An fMRI+ERP study. *Human Brain Mapping 8*(4), 170–181.

Weiler, D. and J. Eggert (2007). Multi-dimensional histogram-based image segmentation. In *Proceedings of the International Conference on Neural Information Processing (ICONIP)*.

Weng, S., H. Wersing, J. J. Steil, and H. Ritter (2006). Learning lateral interactions for feature binding and sensory segmentation from prototypic basis interactions. *IEEE Transactions Neural Networks 17*(4), 843–862.

Wersing, H., J. Eggert, and E. Körner (2003). Sparse coding with invariance constraints. In *International Conference on Artificial Neural Networks ICANN*, pp. 385–392.

Wersing, H., S. Kirstein, M. Götting, H. Brandl, M. Dunn, I. Mikhailova, C. Goerick, J. J. Steil, H. Ritter, and E. Körner (2007). Online learning of objects in a biologically motivated visual architecture. *International Journal of Neural Systems 17*(4), 219–230.

REFERENCES

Wersing, H. and E. Körner (2003). Learning optimized features for hierarchical models of invariant object recognition. *Neural Computation* 15(7), 1559–1588.

Wersing, H., J. J. Steil, and H. Ritter (2001). A competitive layer model for feature binding and sensory segmentation. *Neural Computation* 13(2), 357–387.

Wertheimer, M. (1938). Laws of organization in perceptual forms. In *A source book of gestalt psychology*. London: Routledge and Kegan Paul.

Wojciulik, E. and N. Kanwisher (1999). The generality of parietal involvement in visual attention. *Neuron* 23, 747–764.

Xu, J., X. Chen, and X. Huang (2008). Interactive image segmentation by semi-supervised learning ensemble. In *Proceedings of the International Symposium on Knowledge Acquisition and Modeling*, pp. 645–648.

Yu, S. X. and J. Shi (2003). Object-specific figure-ground segregation. In *Proceedings of IEEE Conference on Computer Vision and Pattern Recognition (CVPR)*, Volume 2, pp. 39–45.

Yu, S. X. and J. Shi (2004). Segmentation given partial grouping constraints. *IEEE Transactions on Pattern Analysis and Machine Intelligence* 26(2), 173–183.

Zhang, H., J. E. Fritts, and S. A. Goldman (2008). Image segmentation evaluation: A survey of unsupervised methods. *Computer Vision and Image Understanding* 110(2), 260–280.

Zhaoping, L. (2005). Border ownership from intracortical interactions in visual area V2. *Neuron* 47, 143–153.

Zhou, H., H. S. Friedman, and R. V. D. Heydt (2000). Coding of border ownership in monkey visual cortex. *Journal of Neuroscience* 20, 6594–6611.

Zhu, S. C. and A. Yuille (1996). Region competition: Unifying snakes, region growing, and bayes/mdl for multiband image segmentation. *IEEE Transactions on Pattern Analysis and Machine Intelligence* 18(9), 884–900.

REFERENCES

Appendix E

Acknowledgments

This work was realized in a joint collaboration with the Cognitive Robotics Lab (CoR-Lab) at Bielefeld University and the Honda Research Institute GmbH (HRI-EU). This was an amazing opportunity to research on an exciting topic under excellent working conditions. Therefore I would like to thank all people who made this experience possible and gave me ongoing support during the past five years. First of all I would like to thank Jochen Steil and Helge Ritter, who already accompanied me during my diploma thesis, initiate the collaboration with the HRI-EU and finally support this thesis until its successful end. In this sense I also want to thank Heiko Wersing, my supervisor at the HRI, for the chance to work at this institute, his ongoing support, helpful advice and the large degree of freedom to follow my scientific interest. Next I also want to thank my colleagues at both institutes who made this time a very good experience in a collaborative and friendly atmosphere. I will miss the interesting discussions and activities in our common time. Here I want to emphasize my regards for my colleagues from the former group "Learning of Sensory Representation", namely Stephan Kirstein, Stephan Hasler, Samuel John and Mathias Franzius. Additionally I would like also to thank them for their support on my thesis by additional experiments, a lot of helpful comments and discussion beyond the scope of our work. Beside many other colleagues I also want to highlight the support provided by the Administration and Software Development teams at the HRI which supply appropriate resources and technical basis that allow me to concentrate on the scientific work. For her scientific collaboration, active support during my work on this thesis and ongoing motivation, I would like to thank my colleague and beloved girlfriend Irene. Finally I would also like to thank all people that accompanied me on the way to the presented work, my friends and my family for their support.

Reprint of the approved thesis submitted to the Faculty of Technology, Bielefeld University, on December 15th, 2010. Date of disputation and approval: February 23th, 2011.

Examiners:
Prof. Dr. Jochen Jakob Steil, CoR-Lab, Bielefeld University
Dr. Heiko Wersing, Honda Research Institute Europe GmbH
Prof. Dr. Michael Biehl, University of Groningen

Examination committee:
Prof. Dr. Robert Giegerich, Bielefeld University
Dr. Marko Tscherepanow, Bielefeld University

i want morebooks!

Buy your books fast and straightforward online - at one of world's fastest growing online book stores! Environmentally sound due to Print-on-Demand technologies.

Buy your books online at
www.get-morebooks.com

Kaufen Sie Ihre Bücher schnell und unkompliziert online – auf einer der am schnellsten wachsenden Buchhandelsplattformen weltweit! Dank Print-On-Demand umwelt- und ressourcenschonend produziert.

Bücher schneller online kaufen
www.morebooks.de

VDM Verlagsservicegesellschaft mbH
Heinrich-Böcking-Str. 6-8
D - 66121 Saarbrücken

Telefon: +49 681 3720 174
Telefax: +49 681 3720 1749

info@vdm-vsg.de
www.vdm-vsg.de

Printed by Books on Demand GmbH, Norderstedt / Germany